Cook the Indian Way
Easy Steps to Everyday Cooking

by NEERA SHARMA

Cook The Indian Way
Easy Steps to Everyday Cooking

Copyright © 2014 by Neera Sharma
All rights reserved.
No part of this book may be reproduced or transmitted in any form or by any means, electronic or mechanical, including photocopying, recording, or by any information storage and retrieval system, without permission in writing from the Author and Publisher, Neera Sharma.

Written, Photographed, Designed, Edited and Self-Published by the Author, Neera Sharma.

Book language; English, with translations of the main ingredients to Hindi.

ISBN-13: 978-1490567099
ISBN: 10:1490567097

DEDICATION

This book is dedicated to my mother, Satya Wati Sharma, who was my role model, and from whom I learned cooking. She was a strong and amazing woman, and an outstanding cook. To my father, Dr. Triloki Nath Sharma–my mentor, who enriched me with worldly knowledge. To my husband, Vinod Sharma, who believed in me, loved my cooking, and encouraged me to continue doing it. And to my children, Ananta, Ruchi and Swaraj, who are my best friends, and the reason I am here today.

THANK YOU

I want to thank my children for always believing in me, loving and tasting my food with honest critique, giving me new ideas and supporting me in writing this book. You are my strength and I love you guys! Also, I want to thank all family and friends who love my cooking and have been waiting for me to complete this book so that they can have it and start cooking my recipes. Many of them would like me to give them cooking lessons; that day will also come soon. Thank you all!

Table of Contents	
	Page No.
Dedication and Thank You	3
Introduction	7
Indian Spices	11
Beverages, Condiments and Relishes	15
Soups, Sandwiches, Pizza and Pasta	33
Yogurt and Rice	51
Lentils and Legumes	66
Vegetable Curries and Snacks	79
Chicken, Fish and Meat	138
Indian Breads	165
Indian Sweets and Baked Treats	180
Menu Ideas	200
Index	205

Introduction

I learned cooking as I grew up watching my mother make delicious food and desserts for family and friends. Along the way, I picked up the secrets of her wonderful cooking.

I am a vegetarian, and have cooked during my entire life, enjoying my time in exploring new recipes, and entertaining my friends and family. Over the past several years, I have been an artist, and a web and graphic designer, but recently, I have realized that cooking is my passion. I want to learn different ways of cooking the same dish, and try to make healthy versions, as much as possible. I like to try cooking new recipes, not only Indian, but from other parts of the world as well. When you read the recipes in this book, you might think that being a vegetarian may limit my cooking. However, I still cook non-vegetarian food. How? It's simple! I just have to know the basics of cooking and the rest comes easily. So, try these recipes. I promise that soon, you will feel like a chef.

I want to mention here that I have designed, photographed, edited, and written this book on my own; and Ananta my daughter, has been guiding me with the editing part, which has been very helpful. For me, this has been a great learning experience, through patience and dedication, and it has been fun as well, that I did it myself!

All recipes in this book are based on what I ate and learned over the years, through experimenting in the kitchen, and creating new ones. I have included all the vegetarian dishes that I love to eat, along with meat, chicken and fish dishes, which I have cooked for friends and family for many years, and which you will make over and over again. These include Lentil and Vegetable Soups, Eggplant Sandwich, Chicken Biryani, Indian Breads, Butter Chicken, Samosas, Coconut Fish Curry, Chicken Pie, and Indian Sweets such as: Rasgoola, Gajar Halwa, and Besan Burfi, to mention a few. Follow the easy steps in these recipes, and you can make a delicious meal! **Remember one important thing; always read the full recipe from start to finish, before making it!**

Now I would like to talk a little bit about my personal background. I was born and raised in India. After I completed my Master's degree in Economics, I got married and moved to Zambia, Africa, with my husband, Vinod Sharma, who was a senior economist in the Copper Mining Company. We had a big house, with elegant Victorian style furniture and a huge kitchen, which was my favorite place in the whole house. Vinod loved to eat good food, and I loved to cook, so we were a good team. We also liked to invite people over, so we would plan parties, and I would cook for large gatherings, especially on our children's birthdays. Once I cooked for approximately two hundred and fifty people! Luckily, I had help from my house keeper Steven, who was a wonderful person.

For large parties, Vinod got five charcoal grills for me, that I could light outside in the backyard and make several dishes at one time. It was amazing! It used to take me one week to prepare for such gatherings, because we always had a large menu along with making cakes for my daughters' birthdays.

Since I was the only cook, it became too hectic for me, so later on I decided to make simpler recipes, that were easier, and took much less time. This gave me a chance to enjoy myself with our guests. It also allowed me time to decorate the house and spend time with my family too!

We had a huge outdoor space and the soil was very fertile, so with the help of Steven, I converted it into a vegetable garden. I grew potatoes, cauliflower, cabbages, carrots, onions, green peppers, eggplants, okra, cilantro, fennel seeds, and even lentils. It was so much fun to cook using these fresh vegetables from the garden. We also had many fruit trees, such as guava, lime, papaya, banana and avocado in our garden. It was like a dream come true–eating fresh vegetables and fruits from my own garden.

In Zambia, it was hard to find Indian restaurants where we could go occasionally to eat, or find ready-made Indian food items. So I had to learn to make many dishes by myself, using trial and error.

Vinod was non-vegetarian and I didn't even want to touch chicken or meat, let alone cooking it at home. He would remove the skin and cut the chicken into small pieces, then I would mix the spices and make the curry. This way I slowly began cooking chicken, then fish, and lastly, meat dishes.

After a lot of experimentation, I came up with some great recipes such as Samosas, Lamb Curry–*Rogan Josh,* Butter Chicken–*Chicken Makhani,* Vegetable Curries, Lentil Soups and all Indian Sweets and Desserts. I also learned to bake cakes and pastries from my best friend, Sarita Bahl. I feel that my time in Africa was well spent because today I am writing this cookbook and sharing my recipes with you all, which makes me feel very happy and proud of myself. You all will do the same one day!!

Everyone likes fresh hot food being served straight from the stove top, so when my friends used to come over, they would stand in the kitchen and I would serve them fresh Jalebi. It is like a hot, crispy mini funnel cake soaked in sugar syrup, and they would enjoy and ask for more until the batter was completely finished.

I am a home body, and for me, home is a place where I am comfortable and cozy, and where my friends and family feel at home, as soon as they walk in the door. It is my place, and I have everything I need to make it my own.

One winter, here in America, the fireplace was lit, keeping the house warm, and fresh flowers spread their perfume. I was cooking in the kitchen—Tandoori Chicken, Cauliflower and Potato Curry, Rice Pilaf, Yogurt Raita, Simple Salad, Fresh Naan; and for desserts–Carrot Halwa and Trifle. I was talking to everyone in the living room, while they were drinking wine and beer, and enjoying themselves. Now, that's what I call home!

Money and Time Saving Tips:
Usually my pantry is full with all the spices, lentils, rice, pasta, flour, semolina and other raw materials, as well as vegetables, fruits, juices and everything else in the fridge. You know what I am talking about. This is my way of living, and I like it.

If my fridge is empty, I turn to my pantry, and take out those things which have not been cooked for a long time—this way they get used, and I save money and time for grocery shopping, which is wonderful in this economy! Isn't that great? Try it and you will feel good about yourself!

Sometimes, I cook with whatever I have at home. It doesn't have to be the exact ingredients I need. This way a new recipe is born, and things get used as well.

Another thing I do to save time is write the ingredients and the measures of my new recipe right away in a notebook, which I keep handy in the kitchen. This way I don't forget what I have done, and don't have to waste time remembering them later on.

In cooking there is no hard and fast rule—you cook based on what you like. Just go with that idea and create something. It will be good; trust me! One day, I made cottage cheese to make palak paneer–*spinach cottage cheese curry*, but I ended up making an Indian dessert called Rasgoola–*sweet cottage cheese dumplings*, because I was craving it. So get started and have fun with cooking!!

Note: **I have used the US Imperial System for measurements.**

Indian Masale
(Indian Spices)

Indian Masale–*Indian Spices,* consists of a large variety, which have been grown across the Indian subcontinent for centuries, depending on the climate in different parts of India.

The most popular spices are: Asafoetida–*Heeing*, Bay Leaf–*Tej Patta*, Black Cardamom–*Badi Ilaichi*, Blue Lichen–*Dagad Phool*, Cinnamon–*Dalchini*, Clove–*Laung*, Coriander–*Dhaniya*, Cumin–*Zeera*, Curry Leaf–*Kadi Patta*, Fennel Seeds–*Saunf*, Fenugreek Seeds–*Methi Beej*, Ginger–*Adrak*, Green Cardamom–*Choti Ilaichi*, Green Chili–*Hari Mirch*, Jaggery–*Gur*, Mace–*Javitri*, Mixed Spice–*Garam Masala*, Mango Powder–*Amchoor*, Mustard Seeds–*Rai*, Nutmeg–*Jaiphal*, Roasted Cumin–*Bhuna Zeera*, Tamarind–*Imli*, Turmeric–*Haldi*, Whole Peppercorn–*Sabut Kali Mirch*,

These are some of the spices I use often, and are commonly used in Indian homes. An extensive list of spices will be too long for me to include here, since they are used in different cuisines, based on various regions of India. Some of the spices, such as fresh garam masala, I make in bulk at home. It lasts me six months, and stays fresh in an airtight jar. Everyone has their own blend of garam masala which brings the difference in the taste in their dishes. Sometimes I grind whole spices and store them separately, and when I need garam masala, I mix small quantities depending on how much I need at that time, so it stays fresh and instant, and brings amazing flavor to all the dishes. You can do the same, and you will see the difference in your cooking.

Image 'Indian Masale' P12: *clockwise, right to left:* green cardamom, green chili, cilantro leaves, ginger, coriander seeds, mint leaves, cumin seeds, and dry red whole chili.

Image 'Sabut Garam Masala' P12: *clockwise, right to left:* whole peppercorns, black cardamom, bay leaves, mace flower, cloves, star anise, blue lichen, cinnamon sticks, and coriander seeds.

Indian Masale *(Indian Spices) Description on P11*

Sabut Garam Masala *(Whole Mixed Spice) Description on P11*

Garam Masala
(Mixed Spice)

Garam Masala is a blend of different spices, called *mixed spice,* and an important ingredient used in Indian cuisine. It is very strong-highly aromatic, and brings out a great flavor in every dish-both meat and vegetarian. It is an expensive spice to buy, so people make it in bulk at home with different combinations of spices and store it in jars. This gives it a long shelf life-thus making it better in flavor.

Makes 2 Cups
Ingredients:
1 cup Coriander Seeds *(Dhaniya)*
2 tablespoons Cumin Seeds *(Zeera)*
2 Bay Leaves *(Tej Patta)*
1 teaspoon Cloves *(Laung)*
2 Cinnamon Sticks *(Dalchini)*
1 Star Anise *(Chakri Phool)*
3 Black Cardamoms *(Badi Ilaichi)*
1 teaspoon Whole Peppercorns *(Sabut Kali Mirch)*
3 Red Whole Round Chilies *(Sabut Gol Lal Mirch)*
3 Mace Flowers *(Javitri Phool)*
1 Blue Lichen *(Dagad Phool)*
1 tablespoon Ginger Powder *(Pisa Adrak)*
Also Needed: Non-Stick Pan, Wooden Spoon

Prep Time: 10 minutes
Cooking Time: 15 minutes
Inactive Time: 40 minutes

Method:
Heat the non-stick pan over low-medium heat, then dry roast all the spices together, except ginger powder and blue lichen, until aromatic and well browned, for about 8-10 minutes.

Keep stirring the spices with the wooden spoon to brown evenly, and prevent burning. Turn off the heat and transfer spices into a bowl. Set aside for 20 minutes to cool completely.

Grind them all together, along with blue lichen, in a coffee grinder. Transfer the spice mix back into the bowl to further cool completely, for about 20 minutes.

Then, mix in the ginger powder. Store it in a clean jar with an airtight lid. Always use a clean dry spoon to take out the spice mix from the jar, then reclose tightly.

Bhuna Zeera
(Roasted Cumin Powder)

Bhuna Zeera is *roasted cumin powder*, which I use in almost all of my cooking, because it brings a smoky flavor to the dish. It can also be made in bulk, like garam masala, or made fresh when you need it.

Makes 1½ Cups
Ingredients:
1 cup Cumin Seeds *(Zeera)*
Also Needed:
Non-Stick Pan or Cast Iron Griddle *(Tava)*
Coffee Grinder, Wooden Spoon

Prep Time: 5 minutes
Cooking Time: 10 minutes
Inactive Time: 30 minutes

Method:
Heat the pan over medium heat and add cumin seeds to it. With the wooden spoon, keep stirring the seeds for even roasting and to prevent burning them, for about 5 minutes, until they are dark brown–black in color, and aromatic.

Turn off the heat and transfer the cumin seeds into a bowl to cool, for about 30 minutes. Grind in a coffee grinder and store in an airtight jar.

Pisa Aur Sabut Bhuna Zeera *(Roasted Cumin Powder and Whole)*

Beverages, Condiments and Relishes

Indian beverages are easy to make; they are good for your health, very refreshing and are enjoyed throughout the year. Popular beverages include Yogurt Smoothie–*Dahi Lassi*, Mango Smoothie–*Aam Ki Lassi*, Fresh Lemonade–*Neembu Pani*, Cumin Water–*Jal Zeera Pani* and Carrot Beverage–*Gajar Ki Kanji*, which is traditionally prepared during the Holi festival in India, around the month of March, and is prepared from purple carrots; then fermented.

My mother made different condiments and relishes every day to go with meals. You will find them in every Indian home or restaurant because no meal is considered complete without condiments and relishes. They bring additional flavors to the main dish and have been traditionally made for many years. My favorite condiments and relishes are: Mint Chutney–*Podiney Ki Chutney*, Tamarind Chutney–*Imli Ki Chutney*, Mango Chutney–*Aam Ki Chutney*, Tomato Chutney–*Timatar Ki Chutney*, Onion Relish–*Pyaz Ka Lachcha*, and Radish Relish–*Mooli Lachcha*.

Aam Ki Lassi
(Mango Smoothie)

Aam Ki Lassi, also called *mango smoothie*, is prepared from mango pulp, yogurt, and milk. It is very refreshing during the summers but can also be enjoyed throughout the year.

Serves 4
Ingredients:

Prep Time: 15 minutes
Cooking Time: 10 minutes

2 ripe, Firm Mangoes *(Aam)*–peeled, pitted and diced
2 cups Plain Low-Fat Yogurt *(Dahi)*
½ cup 2% Milk *(Doodh)*
½ cup Sugar *(Chini)*–add more as needed
pinch of Salt *(Namak)*
1 cup Ice Cubes

Method:
Combine all the above ingredients in a blender, then puree them until smooth. Pour in tall glasses and serve. Adjust sugar to taste.

Aam Ki Lassi *(Mango Smoothie) Recipe on P15*

Open Tomato Sandwich

Aloo Tikki Sandwich *(Potato Cutlet Sandwich) Recipe on P42*

Aloo Tikki Sandwich
(Potato Cutlet Sandwich)

Aloo Tikki Sandwich is my favorite *potato cutlet sandwich*. It is delicious, full of flavor, and satisfying, and can be eaten as a light lunch, or dinner. Potato cutlets can be eaten on their own, as a snack with mint chutney.

Serves 4, Makes 8 *Prep Time: 1 hour*
Ingredients: *Cooking Time: 20 minutes*

2 tablespoons Olive Oil *(Jaitoon Ka Tel)*
8 Slices of Wheat or White Bread
½ cup Tomato Ketchup
½ cup Mint Chutney *(Podina Chutney)*–Refer to Recipe on P24
4 Lettuce Leaves–washed and dried
4 Tomato Slices *(Timatar)*
8-10 Red Onion Rings *(Lal Pyaz)*–pickled in lemon juice and salt
pinch of Crushed Red Pepper *(Kuti Lal Mirch)*–to sprinkle
pinch of Salt *(Namak)*–to sprinkle
pinch of Ground Black Pepper *(Pisi Kali Mirch)*–to sprinkle
4 Potato Cutlets *(Aloo Tikki)*–Refer to Recipe on P113
2 tablespoons Chopped Cilantro *(Hara Dhaniya)*
2 tablespoons Sliced Scallions *(Hara Pyaz)*

Method:

Toast the bread slices in a toaster, or under the broiler with drizzle of olive oil, for about 1-2 minutes, until lightly golden. Spread tomato ketchup on one slice, and mint chutney on the other.

Place a lettuce leaf on mint chutney bread slice, then a tomato slice, 2 onion rings, and sprinkle of crushed red pepper, salt, black pepper to taste. Top it with a potato cutlet, some cilantro, and scallions. Place the tomato ketchup slice on top. Gently press and cut diagonally to make two triangle sandwiches. Repeat until all are done, then serve.

Variations:

-Substitute bread slices with hamburger buns, then prepare the *potato burger*. Keep the other ingredients as same.

-Change the shape of potato cutlet from round to long, just like a hot dog; then prepare a *vegetarian hot dog* with some mustard, and chopped pickled jalapeno on top.

Subzi Pizza
(Vegetable Garden Pizza)

Subzi Pizza is light, juicy and flavorful, with a moist and crispy crust. For this recipe, I have prepared the crust without yeast, and this is my twist on the regular recipe. This will make two deep dish pizzas.

Serves 8
Ingredients:
For Crust:

Prep Time: 40 minutes
Cooking Time: 35 minutes
Inactive Time: 12 hours 15 minutes

2 cups All-Purpose Flour *(Maida)*
2 teaspoons Baking Powder
½ teaspoon Baking Soda
1 teaspoon Salt *(Namak)*
1 cup Plain Yogurt *(Dahi)*
2 tablespoons Warm Water
6 tablespoons Olive Oil *(Jaitoon Ka Tel)*–divided

For Garlic Oil:
3 big Cloves Garlic *(Lehsun)*–grated
¼ teaspoon Crushed Red Pepper *(Kuti Lal Mirch)*
3 tablespoons Olive Oil *(Jaitoon Ka Tel)*

For Toppings:
1 cup cleaned and Chopped Button Mushrooms *(Khumbi)*–sautéed in oil
1 tablespoon Olive Oil *(Jaitoon Ka Tel)*–for sautéing mushrooms
½ cup Chopped Green and Red Bell Peppers *(Shimla Mirch)*
½ cup Cubed Tomatoes *(Timatar)*
1 cup Thinly Sliced Red Onions *(Pyaz)*
8 ounce pack Grated Mozzarella Cheese or 2 cups freshly grated
2 teaspoons Crushed Red Pepper *(Kuti Lal Mirch)*
1 teaspoon Salt *(Namak)*
1 tablespoon Olive Oil *(Jaitoon Ka Tel)*

Method:
Combine flour, baking powder, baking soda, salt, yogurt, water, and 4 tablespoons oil in a large bowl, then mix, and knead, until smooth dough forms; for about 5 minutes. Brush with remaining oil, then cover, and set aside in a warm place, overnight.

Tip: Place the dough in the oven without turning it on. Just turn on the light and it will create enough heat, to help the dough rise faster.

Place the dough on a floured surface, then knead for 10 minutes, until smooth and elastic. Divide it into two equal portions.

With a rolling pin, roll one portion into a 9 by 9 inch round, and the other into a 9 by 9 inch square shape. Transfer each into a round and a square pregreased pan *(with remaining 1 tablespoon oil)* respectively. Use your fingers to pull and spread the dough evenly to cover the base of the pans. Cover for 15 minutes, to rise again.

Meanwhile, prepare the *garlic oil* by mixing garlic, crushed red pepper and oil, in a small pan, and simmer for 5 minutes, until aromatic. Let the garlic oil cool for 5 minutes; then brush it on the pizza crusts.

Spread the **First** thin layer of cheese over the crusts; then a single layer of sautéed mushrooms, with a sprinkle of crushed red pepper and salt, and another thin layer of cheese.

For the **Second** layer, spread green and red peppers evenly, with a little sprinkle of crushed red pepper and salt, and a thin layer of cheese.

For the **Third** layer, spread the tomatoes with a sprinkle of crushed red pepper and salt, and a thin layer of cheese. Adjust the crushed red pepper to your taste.

Spread the onions for the **Fourth** and **final** layer, then sprinkle with crushed red pepper and salt. Top it with remaining cheese, and a drizzle of olive oil.

Bake in a preheated oven at 350 degrees F, for 30 minutes, then turn off the oven. Turn on the broiler, and broil the pizzas for 2 minutes, until the crust is crispy golden and the cheese is bubbly.

Remove pizzas, and wait for a few minutes, then loosen them from the edges of the pan, and slide on to a cutting board. Cut each pizza into 4 slices, then transfer them on to a serving platter. Garnish with a little more crushed red pepper *(optional)*, and eat while still hot.

Variations:
-For *Eggplant-Spinach Pizza*–Baingan Palak Pizza, substitute mushrooms and bell peppers with baby spinach and grilled eggplant slices, then top it with cheddar cheese.
-For *Yeast Pizza Dough*, substitute baking powder and baking soda with 2 teaspoons yeast, and ½ teaspoon sugar in ½ cup warm milk. Knead and set aside for 4 hours in a warm place.

Round Subzi Pizza
(Round Garden Pizza)

Square Subzi Pizza.
(Square Garden Pizza)

Baingan Palak Pizza
(Eggplant Spinach Pizza)

Alfredo Florentine
(Spinach Pasta in White Sauce)

Alfredo Florentine is *spinach pasta in white sauce*, with no cheese, which makes it lighter–keeping the same taste and deliciousness. It is a quick fix, and takes very little effort. Try it in your own kitchen, and you will like it, as much as I do.

Serves 6
Ingredients:

Prep Time: 15 minutes
Cooking Time: 50 minutes

For Sautéed Vegetables:
2 tablespoons Olive Oil *(Jaitoon Ka Tel)*
1 big Onion *(Pyaz)*–chopped
10 ounce pack Frozen Spinach *(Palak)*–thawed
2 tablespoons Water
1 cup Chopped Mini Sweet Peppers *(Choti Shimla Mirch)*
¼ teaspoon Salt *(Namak)*
¼ teaspoon Crushed Red Pepper *(Kuti Lal Mirch)*
2 tablespoons Chopped Cilantro *(Hara Dhaniya)*–divided

For White Sauce:
2 tablespoons Unsalted Butter *(Makkhan)*
2 tablespoons All-Purpose Flour *(Maida)*
1 cup Whole Milk *(Doodh)*
¼ teaspoon Salt *(Namak)*
½ teaspoon Crushed Red Pepper *(Kuti Lal Mirch)*

For Pasta:
1 pound box of Angel Hair Spaghetti
1 Deep Big Pot of Boiling Water
3 tablespoons Salt *(Namak)*
2 tablespoons Canola Oil
1 cup Pasta Water saved

For Garnish: 1 tablespoon Melted Unsalted Butter *(Makkhan)*

Method:

For Vegetables: Heat oil over medium heat in a skillet. Add onions, and sauté for 5 minutes, until translucent. Squeeze the spinach to remove the water, then add it to the onions. Sprinkle a little water on top, and sauté for 10 minutes, over low-medium heat, until soft.

Add mixed sweet peppers, with some salt and crushed red pepper, then sauté for 3-5 minutes, or until tender, but still crunchy, and holding their shapes. Set aside to cool.

For White Sauce–*Bechamel Sauce:* Melt 2 tablespoons of butter over medium-low heat in a heavy base saucepan. Add flour to it, then whisk and cook, for 3 minutes, stirring constantly, until the raw taste of flour minimizes. This process is called making the 'Roux'–*flour and fat mix*.

Whisk in the milk, until smooth, with no lumps. Add salt, and crushed red pepper, then continue to cook, stirring constantly, for 2 minutes, until the sauce is thick and coats the back of a spoon. Turn off the heat.

Add sautéed vegetables and 1 tablespoon cilantro, to the sauce, then gently fold them in, until just combined. Check the seasoning, and add more as needed.

To Boil Pasta: Meanwhile, heat water in a large pot, over medium-high heat, until it comes to a boil, about 10 minutes. Season the water with salt and oil, then add pasta to it. Give it a good stir, and let pasta cook for about 10-12 minutes, until firmly cooked–*al dente*.

Save a cup of pasta water to use later, then strain the pasta, and add it to the white sauce. Toss it with kitchen tongs to combine everything well. If pasta is too dry, add a little of the saved pasta water, and toss again.

Transfer Alfredo Florentine into a serving dish. Garnish with remaining cilantro and 1 tablespoon melted butter, then serve hot.

Alfredo Florentine *(Spinach Pasta in White Sauce)*

Baingan Lasagna
(Eggplant Lasagna)

Baingan Lasagna is *eggplant lasagna* prepared from whole wheat lasagna noodles, eggplant, fresh tomato sauce, and cheese.

Serves 6　　　　　　　　　　*Prep Time: 20 minutes*
Ingredients:　　　　　　　　*Cooking Time: 2 hours 20 minutes*
Toppings:

1 medium Eggplant *(Baingan)*–cut into ¼ inch thick round slices
3½ cups Grated Mozzarella Cheese
2 tablespoons Olive Oil *(Jaitoon Ka Tel)*
Salt *(Namak)* and Black Pepper *(Kali Mirch)*–to taste

For Tomato Sauce:
4 tablespoons Olive Oil *(Jaitoon Ka Tel)*–divided
3 medium Onions *(Pyaz)*–finely chopped
2 large Tomatoes *(Timatar)*–finely chopped
½ cup Tomato Juice *(Timatar Rus)*
½ cup Tomato Ketchup
1 cup Chopped Mini Sweet Peppers *(Choti Shimla Mirch)*
2 tablespoons Chopped Cilantro *(Hara Dhaniya)*
2 tablespoons Chopped Mint Leaves *(Podina)*
1 teaspoon Minced Green Chili *(Hari Mirch)*
1½ teaspoons Salt *(Namak)*
¼ teaspoon Red Chili Powder *(Lal Mirch)*
2 teaspoons Roasted Cumin Powder *(Bhuna Zeera)*
½ teaspoon Ginger Powder *(Pisa Adrak)*

To Boil Lasagna Noodles:
A Deep Big Pot of Boiling Water
3 tablespoons Salt *(Namak)*
2 tablespoons Canola Oil
13.25 ounce box of Whole Wheat Lasagna Noodles
Big Bowl of Cold Water with Ice

Method:
Spread the eggplant slices on a sheet pan, and sprinkle some salt and pepper to taste, then drizzle with 2 tablespoons oil. With clean hands, massage the slices to evenly coat with oil.

Bake the eggplant slices in a preheated oven at 350 degrees F, for 20-25 minutes, until golden, and cooked through. Check with a tooth pick, then remove and set aside to cool.

Meanwhile heat oil in a medium saucepan, over medium heat, then add onions and sauté for 6-8 minutes, until golden.

Add the remaining ingredients for the *sauce*, then cover and cook for 15 minutes, over low-medium heat, stirring often, until tomatoes are soft and mushy; the oil separates, and the sauce thickens. Set aside to cool.

Cook noodles in the boiling water, seasoned with salt and oil, for 10-12 minutes, until firmly cooked–*al dente*.

Quickly strain the pasta and transfer it into the ice cold water, to stop the cooking process. This is called *'shocking'*. It keeps the shape of noodles firm and intact.

For the **First** layer, spread the tomato sauce, then the noodles length-ways, in an oval pregreased baking dish to cover the base.

For the **Second** layer, spread the tomato sauce again. For the **Third** layer, sprinkle some cheese. For the **Fourth** layer, spread the eggplant slices.

For the **Fifth** layer, spread more cheese. Then, alternate the direction of the noodles; this time width-ways. This keeps the layers intact.

Repeat the first four layers as indicated above, and then cover the top with remaining cheese.

Sprinkle some salt and pepper, and a drizzle of olive oil on top. Bake at 350 degrees F, for 30-40 minutes, until the cheese melts; it is bubbly, and golden on top.

Remove and set aside for 10 minutes. Garnish with cilantro, then cut Baingan Lasagna into slices, and serve hot with mashed potatoes *(P50)*.

Aloo Ka Bhurta
(Mashed Potatoes)

Aloo Ka Bhurta is *mashed potatoes*, prepared from boiled potatoes with lots of flavors added to them. They are lighter, flavorful, and have a kick to them. This is my twist on the traditional recipe.

Serves 6

Ingredients:

Prep Time: 25 minutes
Cooking Time: 15 minutes

1 cup Melted Unsalted Butter *(Makkhan)*
8 ounce (1 cup) Sour Cream
2 teaspoons Salt *(Namak)*
2 teaspoons Crushed Black Pepper *(Kuti Kali Mirch)*
2 tablespoons Fresh Lemon Juice *(Neembu Rus)*
¼ cup Chopped Chives *(Hara Pyaz)*
¼ cup Chopped Cilantro *(Hara Dhaniya)*
1 Green Chili *(Hari Mirch)*–finely chopped (remove seeds for less heat)
12 medium Potatoes *(Aloo)*–boiled, peeled and grated

Method:

In a medium bowl, combine butter, sour cream, salt, pepper, lemon juice, and half each chives, cilantro and green chili, then mix; and add to the potatoes. Gently fold in, until everything combines, and is evenly distributed. Check the seasoning and add more as needed.

Transfer Aloo Ka Bhurta into a serving bowl and garnish with remaining cilantro, chives, and green chili.

Serve warm with steak, chicken, or pasta dishes, or with khichadi–*lentil rice polenta*.

Yogurt and Rice

Yogurt and Rice are important parts of an Indian balanced meal. **Yogurt,** also known as *Dahi* in India, is eaten either plain or in raita form. It is the main ingredient used in making plain, sweet or savory lassi, mango lassi, and dishes like: kadhi pakori, dahi aloo, dahi vada, dahi pakori and different vegetable raitas. Marinades for chicken and meat dishes like: tandoori chicken, chicken tikka masala, meat kebabs are all yogurt based.

Rice, also known as *Chawal* in India, is eaten either plain boiled, or as vegetable pilaf or chicken biryani. For desserts: as rice pudding, and sweet saffron rice–*zarda*. Basmati Chawal, means *Aromatic Long Grain Rice,* and is called *Champagne of India*. It is commonly used in Indian homes and restaurants every day.

Moong Dal Pakori
(Moong Lentil Dumplings)
Recipe on P52

Urad Dal Vada
(Urad Lentil Doughnuts)
Recipe on P55

51

Yogurt

Dahi Saunth Pakori
(Yogurt Tamarind Dumpling)

Dahi Saunth Pakori is *yogurt tamarind dumpling*-popular in north India. The dumplings are prepared from split moong and urad lentils, which are then soaked in yogurt sauce with a drizzle of tamarind chutney.

Serves 8-10
Ingredients:
For Dumplings: Makes 30 Small

Prep Time: 20 minutes
Cooking Time: 30 minutes
Inactive Time: 13 hours

1 cup Split Moong Lentils *(Moong Dhuli)*
¼ cup Split Urad Lentils *(Urad Dhuli)*
3 cups, plus 2 tablespoons Water
1 teaspoon Minced Ginger and Green Chili *(Adrak-Hari Mirch)*
½ teaspoon Salt *(Namak)*
1 tablespoon Chopped Cilantro *(Hara Dhaniya)*
½ teaspoon Baking Soda
1 cup Vegetable Oil–for frying
A Large Bowl with 6 cups Water

For Yogurt Sauce
2½ cups Plain Low-Fat Yogurt *(Dahi)*
½ cup 2% Milk *(Doodh)* or Water
½ teaspoon Salt *(Namak)*
½ teaspoon Red Chili Powder *(Lal Mirch)*
½ teaspoon Roasted Cumin Powder *(Bhuna Zeera)*
½ teaspoon Black Rock Salt *(Kala Namak–pink in color)* (optional)
1 tablespoon Chopped Cilantro *(Hara Dhaniya)*
dash of Red Chili Powder, Cumin Powder–for garnish
1 cup Tamarind Chutney *(Imli Ki Chutney)*–Refer to Recipe on P 27
½ cup Mint Chutney *(Podiney Ki Chutney)*–Refer to Recipe on P 24

Method:

For Moong Dumplings, mix the two lentils in a medium bowl, then rinse them 3-4 times in water, or until the water is clear. Soak the lentils in 3 cups of water overnight. Strain the lentils, then grind them in a blender or a food processor with 2 tablespoons water, until a smooth thick batter forms. Add a few more tablespoons of water if needed.

Transfer the batter into a bowl, and whip by hand or using a hand beater, for 2-3 minutes, until light and fluffy. Whipping helps make lighter dumplings—otherwise they will be dense and heavy. Add ginger-green chili, salt, cilantro, and baking soda, then mix well.

Heat the oil in a wok or karahi–*Indian wok*, over medium heat, until hot. Test by dropping a little batter in the oil, which should sizzle, and rise to the top in 30 seconds, and not turn brown. The oil is ready to use.

With a small ice cream scoop, or by hand, drop the batter equal to 1 teaspoon, into the oil, in batches of 6. The batter will puff up into light round dumplings. Reduce the heat to medium-low, then turn them and fry for 1-2 minutes, until lightly golden on all sides. Adjust the heat temperatures between medium and medium-low, as needed.

Remove the dumplings with a slotted spoon, and drop them into the bowl of water. Repeat, until the batter is finished. Soaking the dumplings in water helps them to soften.

Meanwhile, prepare the *yogurt*. Add milk or water, salt, red chili powder, cumin powder, black rock salt *(optional)*, and half the cilantro to the yogurt, then whisk it to make a smooth sauce.

Take the dumplings, one at a time, and squeeze to remove water, then dip in the yogurt sauce, and arrange in a 9 by 13 by 3 inch deep, glass rectangle or round dish. Pour half the yogurt sauce over the dumplings evenly, and save the rest as extra, to be used as needed.

Garnish with dash of red chili, cumin powder, and remaining cilantro. Cover with a plastic wrap, and refrigerate for 1 hour before serving.

To Serve: Take 2 yogurt dumplings in a small dessert size bowl with a drizzle of tamarind and mint chutney, then serve.

Tip: Prepare the dumplings a day before, and refrigerate without soaking in the water. Then, soak them in hot water, 2 hours before serving, for 10 minutes, until soft.

Variations:
-Serve hot dumplings as a snack with tamarind and mint chutney.
-Use dumplings in the preparation of vegetarian dumplings curry.
-Substitute the lentils with lentil flour, and double its proportion. Prepare the batter as in the recipe above, without the baking soda. Keep the batter in a warm place for 2 hours to ferment. Mix in the baking soda, and then fry the dumplings.

Dahi Saunth Pakori *(Yogurt Tamarind Dumpling) Recipe on P52*

Dahi Vada *(Yogurt Lentil Doughnuts)*

Dahi Vada
(Yogurt Lentil Doughnuts)

Dahi Vada are savory, soft and delicious *yogurt lentil doughnuts*, prepared from split urad and moong lentils batter, then soaked in yogurt sauce. I have been making these doughnuts for many years, and they come out perfect every time.

Serves 12
Ingredients:
For Doughnuts: Makes 24
1½ cups Split Urad Lentils *(Urad Dhuli)*
½ cup Split Moong Lentils *(Moong Dhuli)*
4 cups, plus 2 tablespoons Water–divided
1 teaspoon Minced Ginger and Green Chili *(Adrak-Hari Mirch)*
½ teaspoon Salt *(Namak)*
½ teaspoon Baking Soda
1 tablespoon Chopped Cilantro *(Hara Dhaniya)*
24 Whole Peppercorns *(Sabut Kali Mirch)* (optional)
1 cup, plus 2 tablespoons Vegetable Oil

For Yogurt Sauce:
3 cups Plain Low-Fat Yogurt *(Dahi)*
½ cup 2% Milk *(Doodh)* or Water
½ teaspoon Salt *(Namak)*
½ teaspoon Red Chili Powder *(Lal Mirch)*
½ teaspoon Black Rock Salt *(Kala Namak-pink in color)* (optional)
1 teaspoon Roasted Cumin Powder *(Bhuna Zeera)*

For Garnish:
dash of Roasted Cumin *(Bhuna Zeera)* and Red Chili *(Lal Mirch)* Powder
drizzle of Tamarind *(Imli)* and Mint *(Podina)* Chutney

Prep Time: 20 minutes
Cooking Time: 45 minutes
Inactive Time: 12 hours

Method:
For Doughnut Batter, mix the two lentils in a medium bowl, and rinse 3-4 times in water, or until the water is clear. Soak them in 3 cups water, overnight. Strain the lentils, then grind them in a blender or a food processor with 2 tablespoons water, until a smooth thick batter forms. Add 1-2 tablespoons more water if needed.

Transfer the batter into a bowl, and whip by hand or a hand beater, for 2-3 minutes, until light and fluffy. Whipping helps make lighter doughnuts—otherwise they will be dense and heavy. Add ginger-green chili, salt, baking soda, and half the cilantro to the batter, then mix well.

Heat 1 cup of oil in a karahi or a wok over low-medium heat. Test by dropping a little batter in the oil, which should sizzle and rise to the top in 30 seconds, and not turn brown. The oil is ready to fry.

Lightly wet your left palm using the remaining 1 cup water, then scoop out 1 tablespoon of batter with your right hand and place it on the left wet pam. Insert a peppercorn in the center of the batter *(optional)*. *The peppercorn gives an extra burst of heat and flavor to the doughnut.*

Lightly pat the batter with wet fingers of your right hand, to make it flat and round. Then, with a wet finger, make a hole in the center of the round, like a doughnut. Carefully lift it, and slide into the hot oil.

Add 3 more doughnuts to the oil to make 4, then fry for 2 minutes on each side, until lightly golden. Remove with a slotted spoon, and transfer them on to a plate, lined with a paper towel, to drain excess oil. Cover with another paper towel to prevent drying. Repeat, and fry the remaining doughnuts, until the batter is finished.

Note: Do not flip over the doughnuts too many times, while frying, as they will soak up too much oil.

Tip: You can also make the doughnuts on a plastic sheet. Brush some oil on it, then scoop a tablespoon of batter, and place on the plastic. Brush a little oil on top. Lightly pat and make a hole, then fry as shown above.

To Assemble Dahi Vada: Combine and whisk yogurt, and milk or water, in a bowl, until smooth. Add salt, red chili powder, cumin powder, black rock salt *(optional)*, and some cilantro, then mix well. Place two warm doughnuts in a dessert size bowl, then pour 6 tablespoons yogurt sauce on top, until they are soaked in it. Sprinkle a dash of cumin and red chili powder, and drizzle some tamarind and mint chutney, then serve.

Variations:
-Serve lentil doughnut as a snack with mint and tamarind chutney or with Sāmbhar–a south Indian lentil soup.
-Substitute lentils with lentil flour, and double its proportion. Prepare the batter as in the recipe above, without the baking soda. Keep the batter in a warm place for 2 hours to ferment. Mix in the baking soda, then fry the doughnuts.

Kheera Raita
(Cucumber Yogurt Sauce)

Raita is *yogurt sauce,* prepared from yogurt and vegetables, such as cucumber, potato, tomato, onion, and bottle gourd, or any other vegetable of your choice. It is a popular food item in Indian cuisine and very refreshing in the summer time.

Serves 6
Ingredients:

Prep Time: 15 minutes
Cooking Time: 10 minutes
Inactive Time: 1 hour

3 cups Plain Non-Fat Yogurt *(Dahi)*
1 cup 2% Milk *(Doodh)* or Water
¼ teaspoon Black Rock Salt *(Kala Namak-pink in color)* *(optional)*
1 teaspoon Salt *(Namak)*
½ teaspoon Red Chili Powder *(Lal Mirch)*
1 teaspoon Roasted Cumin Powder *(Bhuna Zeera)*
2 English Cucumbers *(Kheera)*
2 tablespoons Chopped Cilantro *(Hara Dhaniya)*–divided
dash of Red Chili *(Lal Mirch)* and Roasted Cumin *(Zeera)* Powder

Method:
In a medium bowl, combine yogurt and milk or water, then whisk, until a smooth sauce has formed. Add black and white salt, red chili, and cumin powder, then mix well. Set aside for later use.

In another bowl, peel and grate the cucumbers, then squeeze to remove all their water content; and combine with half the cilantro. Add the yogurt sauce to the cucumber, and mix, to incorporate everything well

Cover the sauce with a plastic wrap, and refrigerate for 1 hour before serving. Garnish with remaining cilantro, a dash of red chili powder, and cumin powder. Then, serve Kheera Raita as an accompaniment to vegetable pilaf or chicken biryani, or an entire meal.

Variations:
-*Vegetable Yogurt Sauce*–*Subzi Raita:* Substitute grated cucumber with chopped–1 red onion, 1 firm tomato, and ½ peeled cucumber–all of medium size. Add vegetables to the yogurt sauce, then mix and serve.

-*Mint Yogurt Sauce*–*Podina Raita:* Substitute grated cucumber with the puree of 1 cup fresh mint leaves, or ¼ cup dry mint leaves; crushed into powder, then mixed in yogurt sauce.

-*Potato Yogurt Sauce*–Aloo Raita: Substitute grated cucumber with 2 medium boiled potatoes; peeled and cubed, plus ½ cup milk.

-*Bottle Gourd Yogurt Sauce*–Ghiya Raita: Substitute grated cucumber with small bottle gourd–peeled, grated, boiled, strained and squeezed; to remove all its water content. Mix in the yogurt sauce. Serve chilled.

-*Gram Flour Puffs Yogurt Sauce*–Boondi Raita: Substitute grated cucumber with ½ cup boondi–*fried gram flour puffs;* soaked in warm water. Strain, and mix in the yogurt sauce. Serve chilled.

-*Serving Suggestion:* Serve as a dip with snacks and chips.

Kheera Raita
(Cucumber Yogurt Sauce)
Recipe on P57

Aloo Khumbi Pulao
(Potato Mushroom Pilaf)

Aloo Khumbi Pulao
(Potato Mushroom Pilaf)

Aloo Khumbi Pulao is a flavorful *potato mushroom pilaf*, prepared from rice, mushrooms, potatoes, Indian spices, and flavorings. For this recipe, I have used button mushrooms, but you can use any kind you prefer.

Serves 6 *Prep Time: 20 minutes*
Ingredients: *Cooking Time: 45 minutes*

1½ cups Basmati Rice *(Basmati Chawal)*
¾ cup Warm Tap Water (reduces cooking time)
pinch of Saffron *(Zafran)*
3 tablespoons Olive Oil *(Jaitoon Ka Tel)*
½ cup Minced Onion *(Pyaz)*
1 big Clove Garlic *(Lehsun)*–grated
1 tablespoon Minced Ginger and Green Chili *(Adrak-Hari Mirch)*
½ teaspoon Turmeric Powder *(Haldi)*
2½ teaspoons Salt *(Namak)*
½ teaspoon Red Chili Powder *(Lal Mirch)*
½ teaspoon Roasted Cumin Powder *(Bhuna Zeera)*
½ teaspoon Mixed Spice *(Garam Masala)*
1 cup cleaned and Finely Chopped Button Mushrooms *(Khumbi)*
2 medium Potatoes *(Aloo)*–peeled, diced, and half boiled (in microwave)
½ cup Diced Mini Sweet Peppers *(Choti Shimla Mirch)*
1 tablespoon Chopped Cilantro *(Hara Dhaniya)*, plus Scallions *(Hara Pyaz)*

Method:
Gently rinse the rice in water, 3-4 times, or until the water is clear, then soak it in only ¾ cup of water, for 10 minutes. Since the vegetables also release water; using less water, results into fluffy rice.

Meanwhile, heat oil in a wok, over medium heat, then add onions, and sauté, for 6-8 minutes, until golden. Add garlic, and ginger-green chili, and stir-fry for a minute, until fragrant. Reduce the heat to low-medium, and add turmeric, salt, red chili, cumin powder, and mixed spice, then cook for a minute, until oil separates.

Add mushrooms, and sauté for 2-3 minutes, until tender and lightly golden. Add potatoes, and peppers, then sauté for another 2 minutes. Add rice, along with the soaking water, and saffron. Gently stir, being careful not to break the rice. Increase the heat to medium, until the water comes to a boil.

Reduce the heat back to low-medium. Cover and cook for 10-15 minutes, until most of the water evaporates. Reduce the heat to low, and allow the rice to simmer–still covered, for 5 minutes, until completely cooked.

Turn off the heat, and wait for 10 minutes. Then uncover, and gently fluff the rice, from the edges, with a fork, to release the steam. This keeps every grain of rice separate and intact–and not mushy.

Gently transfer the rice on to a serving platter, then garnish with cilantro and scallions. Serve hot Aloo Khumbi Pulao, with vegetable raita, roasted papadam, and homemade neembu pani–*fresh lemonade*.

Zafrani Chawal
(*Savory Saffron Rice*)

Murg Biryani (*Chicken Pilaf*) Recipe on P62

Zafrani Chawal
(Savory Saffron Rice)

Zafrani Chawal is *savory saffron rice*, prepared from basmati rice, and saffron. It is a great accompaniment to meat and vegetarian curries.

Serves 4
Ingredients:

Prep Time: 15 minutes
Cooking Time: 30 minutes

2 cups Basmati Rice *(Basmati Chawal)*
4 cups Hot Tap Water (reduces cooking time)
½ teaspoon Saffron *(Zafran)*
2 tablespoons Olive Oil *(Jaitoon Ka Tel)*
1 medium Onion *(Pyaz)*–chopped
2 teaspoons Salt *(Namak)*
1 teaspoon Mixed Spice *(Garam Masala)*

For Garnish:
1 tablespoon Chopped Cilantro *(Hara Dhaniya)*
1 tablespoon Thinly Sliced Scallions *(Hara Pyaz)*

Method:
Gently rinse the rice 3-4 times in water, or until the water is clear, then soak it in 4 cups water, with the saffron, for 10 minutes.

Meanwhile, heat the oil in a wide pan over medium heat. Add onions, and sauté, for about 6-8 minutes, until golden brown. Then add salt, mixed spice, and rice, along with the saffron water.

Increase the heat to medium-high, until the water comes to a boil. Then, reduce the heat to low-medium. Cover and cook for 15 minutes, until most of the water evaporates, and the rice cooks through.

Turn off the heat, and leave the rice covered, for 5 minutes, to allow it to simmer in its own steam. Uncover, and gently fluff the rice from the edges with a fork, to release steam, keeping the grains separate and intact.

Serving suggestion: Gently spoon the Zafrani Chawal on to a serving platter, then garnish with cilantro, and scallions. Serve hot with any meat or vegetarian curry.

Murg Biryani
(Chicken Pilaf)

Murg Biryani is a world known dish, which originated from Persia. It is cooked in 'Dum'—meaning—*over low heat*, in a sealed heavy base pot. For this recipe, I have used partially cooked chicken, and raw rice, then cooked them on the stove top. I find that this is the easiest way to prepare Murg Biryani, as the dish is lighter than the original recipe, yet flavorful, with juicy chicken.

Serves 4
Ingredients:

Prep Time: 30 minutes
Cooking Time: 1 hour 20 minutes
Inactive time: 12 hours

For Marinade:
1 cup Plain Greek Yogurt *(Dahi)*
1 teaspoon Salt *(Namak)*
½ teaspoon Ground Black Pepper *(Kali Mirch)*
1½ teaspoons Red Chili Powder *(Lal Mirch)*
1 teaspoon Roasted Cumin Powder *(Bhuna Zeera)*
1 teaspoon Minced Ginger and Green Chili *(Adrak-Hari Mirch)*
3 big Cloves Garlic *(Lehsun)*–grated
2 tablespoons Chopped Cilantro *(Hara Dhaniya)*
2 teaspoons Mixed Spice *(Garam Masala)*
2 tablespoons Lemon Juice *(Neembu Rus)*
½ cup Olive Oil *(Jaitoon Ka Tel)*

Also Needed: 4 skinless boneless Chicken *(Murg)* Breasts (1 pound)

For Cooking Biryani:
2 cups Basmati Rice *(Basmati Chawal)*
2 cups Hot Tap Water (reduces cooking time)
¼ teaspoon Saffron *(Zafran)*
3 tablespoons Olive Oil *(Jaitoon Ka Tel)*–divided
1 medium Onion *(Pyaz)*–chopped
2 tablespoon Chopped Pistachio, Cashews, Almonds *(Pista, Kaju, Badam)*
Medium Heavy Base Pot
Aluminum Foil

For Garnish:
2 tablespoons Chopped Cilantro *(Hara Dhaniya)*
1 tablespoon Unsalted Butter *(Makkhan)*–cut into 4 pieces
½ Lemon *(Neembu)*

Method:

Marinate Chicken: Combine all the ingredients for the marinade in a bowl; then whisk them to a smooth blend. Refrigerate the marinade for 15 minutes, until chicken is ready.

Meanwhile, cut each chicken breast into 3 pieces, making 12 in all. Place the pieces in a plastic container, and pour marinade over them. Stir them around, until well coated, then cover and refrigerate overnight.

Soak Rice: Gently rinse the rice 3-4 times in water, or until the water is clear. Then, soak it in 2 cups water with the saffron, for about 15 minutes. Saffron gives a nice golden color and aroma to the biryani.

Cook Chicken: Heat a grill pan over medium heat, then brush it with 1 tablespoon oil. Shake off the extra marinade, and place 6 chicken pieces on the pan. Grill for 2-3 minutes on each side, until lightly golden, but partially cooked. Remove and set aside to cool. Repeat, and grill the remaining chicken pieces, until all are done.

Cook Biryani: Heat a heavy base medium pot over medium heat. Add the remaining 2 tablespoons oil to it, then add onions and saute for 6-8 minutes, until golden. Reduce heat and add the leftover marinade on top of the onions, then place all the chicken pieces in a single layer. Spread the next layer of dry nuts. Finally, add the soaked rice along with the saffron water, and spread them as evenly as possible, in a single layer.

Cover the pot with foil, tightly around the edges, then place the lid on top, to prevent steam from escaping. Increase the heat to medium-high, and cook for 5 minutes. Then, reduce the heat to low-medium, and place a cast iron griddle under the pot, to prevent from burning. Cook for 20-25 minutes, then turn off the heat. Leave it covered, for 10 minutes, until biryani is fully cooked in its own steam, and smells heavenly.

Carefully remove the lid, and then the foil—watch out for the hot steam escaping! With a fork, fluff the rice from the edges of the pot, to release the steam. Then, move the chicken pieces away from rice.

To Serve Biryani: Spread a layer of rice on a serving platter like a bed, then place the chicken pieces on top, and then another layer of rice. Garnish with cilantro, butter, and a squeeze of lemon juice, then serve hot Murg Biryani with onion relish, and vegetable yogurt sauce.

Khichadi
(Lentil Rice Polenta)

Khichadi is comfort food, prepared from lentils, rice, and added tempering. It is best, when you need a break from heavy meals, or if you are not feeling well. Kichadi is light on the stomach, and digests easily.

Serves 4
Ingredients:

Prep Time: 20 minutes
Cooking Time: 75 minutes

1 cup Mixed Lentils
(Arhar Dhuli, Lal Masoor Dhuli, Sabut Masoor, Moong Chilka)
½ cup Basmati Rice *(Basmati Chawal)*
1 tablespoon Olive Oil *(Jaitoon Ka Tel)*
½ teaspoon Turmeric Powder *(Haldi)*
1½ teaspoons Salt *(Namak)*–add more as needed
6 cups Hot Tap Water (reduces cooking time)

For Tempering:
2 tablespoons Olive Oil *(Jaitoon Ka Tel)*
pinch of Asafoetida *(Heeing)*
¼ teaspoon Cumin Seeds *(Zeera)*
¼ teaspoon Turmeric Powder *(Haldi)*
½ teaspoon Red Chili Powder *(Lal Mirch)*

For Garnish: 1 tablespoon Unsalted Butter *(Makkhan)*

Method:

Combine the mixed lentils and the rice in a bowl, then rinse in water 3-4 times, or until the water is clear. Soak in 6 cups water for 15 minutes.

Meanwhile, heat the oil in a medium heavy base pot over low-medium heat. Then, remove the pot away from heat for a minute, and add turmeric, salt, and lentil-rice mix, along with the soaking water. Stir well to incorporate everything.

Bring the pot back on the heat, and increase it to medium-high. Allow the water to boil, then reduce the heat to low-medium. Cover and cook, for 50 minutes, or until it is thick like a porridge. Stir every 10 minutes to prevent burning. Add more water as needed, until cooked

Turn off the heat, and check the seasoning; add more as needed, then transfer the khichadi into a serving dish and prepare the tempering.

Tempering: Heat oil in a small pan over medium heat. Add asafoetida, and let it sizzle, then add cumin seeds, and let them crackle.

Further, add turmeric, and red chili powder. Give it a quick swirl, and pour over khichadi. Garnish with unsalted butter, for additional flavor, then serve hot Khichadi with mint yogurt sauce, mashed potatoes, onion relish, and papadam.

Variations:
-*For Vegetable Kichadi*: Sauté some vegetables–1 small chopped onion, 1 small potato peeled and cubed, 4 cauliflower florets sliced, 6 green beans sliced, and 2 tablespoons green peas, in 2 tablespoons of olive oil, and a dash of salt, until tender. Add them to the khichadi, just before adding the tempering, and mix. This will add extra flavor to khichadi.

-*For Tempering*: Substitute plain tempering, with onion tempering. Sauté 1 chopped onion, in 2 tablespoons oil, then follow the steps to make the tempering as in the khichadi recipe above.

Khichadi *(Lentil Rice Polenta)*

Lentils and Legumes

Lentils and Legumes are high-protein pulses and beans, that are part of the Indian staple diet, and are eaten with plain boiled rice, or roti. Some of the popular Indian lentils, also called 'Dal', in India are: Yellow Split Moong–*Moong Dhuli*, Green Split Moong–*Moong Chilka*, Yellow Split Arhar–*Arhar Dhuli*, Brown Whole Masoor–*Sabut Masoor*, Red Split Masoor–*Lal Masoor Dhuli*, Black Whole Urad–*Sabut Urad*, and White Split Urad–*Urad Dhuli*.

Red Kidney Beans–*Rajma*, Black Eyed Peas–*Lobhiya*, Black Grams–*Kaale Chaney*, and Chick Peas–*White Choley*, are examples of some of the popular legumes in Indian cuisine.

Lentils can be used in making several food items, such as: lentil soups, dry tempered lentils; batter for lentil dumplings–*pakori*, lentil doughnuts–*vada*, lentil crepes–*dosa*, steamed lentil-rice cake–*idli*, dumplings curry; dough for making papadam; filling for potato cutlets, and stuffed poori–*fried puffed wheat bread*.

Legumes can be used in making curries, salads, hummus, cutlets, healthy snacks or as a filling for gol guppas.

Clockwise Right to Left: Yellow Split Moong, Brown Whole Masoor, Yellow Split Arhar, Green Split Moong, Red Split Masoor, *Center:* Red Kidney Beans

Dal Tadka
(Tempered Lentil Soup)

Dal Tadka is a popular north Indian *tempered lentil soup*, prepared from mixed lentils with added *Tadka*, also known as *Chaunk*, *Baghar* or *Tempering*, on top. Lentils are a ready source of protein, especially for vegetarians, and an important part of Indian cuisine. They are regularly eaten with rice and vegetables, in south India; and with both rice and roti–*whole wheat flatbread*, throughout north India.

Serves 6

Ingredients:

1½ cups Split Arhar Lentils *(Arhar Dhuli)*
½ cup Split Masoor Lentils *(Masoor Dhuli)*
8 cups Hot Tap Water (reduces cooking time)
2 tablespoons Olive Oil *(Jaitoon Ka Tel)*
1 medium Onion *(Pyaz)*–finely chopped
1 big Clove Garlic *(Lehsun)*–grated
1 medium Tomato *(Timatar)*–finely chopped
1 teaspoon Minced Ginger and Green Chili *(Adrak-Hari Mirch)*
½ teaspoon Turmeric Powder *(Haldi)*
2 teaspoons Salt *(Namak)*
2 tablespoons Chopped Cilantro *(Hara Dhaniya)*

For Tempering:

1 tablespoon Olive Oil *(Jaitoon Ka Tel)*
pinch of Asafoetida *(Heeing) (Optional)*
½ teaspoon Cumin Seeds *(Zeera)*
¼ teaspoon Turmeric Powder *(Haldi)*
½ teaspoon Red Chili Powder *(Lal Mirch)*
½ teaspoon Mango Powder *(Amchoor)*

Prep Time: 15 minutes
Cooking Time: 70 minutes
Inactive Time: 15 minutes

Method:

Mix the lentils in a bowl and rinse them in water, 3-4 times, or until the water is clear. Then, soak them in 8 cups of water for 15 minutes.

Meanwhile, heat the oil in a medium pot over medium heat. Add onions, and sauté, for 5 minutes, until lightly golden. Add garlic, and sauté for another minute, then add tomatoes, ginger-green chili, turmeric, and salt, and sauté for 5 more minutes, until the tomatoes are soft. Add soaked lentils, along with the soaking water, and stir well.

Increase the heat to medium-high, until water comes to a boil. Reduce the heat to low-medium; cover and cook for 60 minutes, or until lentils are soft and soup is thicker. Stir occasionally to form even consistency.

Check the seasoning, and add more as needed. Then, add cilantro, and mix again, and transfer the lentil soup into a serving dish.

Plain Tempering–*Sada Chaunk:* Heat oil in a small pan, over medium heat. Add asafoetida, and let it sizzle, then add cumin seeds, and let them crackle. Add turmeric, red chili powder, and mango powder, then give a quick swirl, and pour over the lentil soup. It should have a sizzling sound. Serve hot Dal Tadka with fresh tava roti, or plain rice, accompanied with roasted papadam, and tomato chutney.

Note: Use of asafoetida, in preparing the soup and tempering, helps to release gas caused by lentils, because they are rich in carbohydrates.

Variations:
-Cook with onions and add tomato tempering.
-Cook with tomatoes and add onion tempering.
-Cook with garlic and add tomato-onion tempering.
-Cook plain lentils, and add onion, garlic, and tomato tempering.
-Garnish with lemon juice for some extra freshness, and flavor.

Dal Tadka *(Tempered Lentil Soup)*

Dal Palak
(Lentil Spinach Soup)

Dal Palak is a healthy *lentil spinach soup*, full of flavor and nutrients. It is prepared from split yellow moong lentils and spinach, with added tempering on top. For this recipe, I have used frozen spinach.

Serves 6
Ingredients:

Prep Time: 15 minutes
Cooking Time: 45 minutes
Inactive Time: 15 minutes

1 cup Split Moong Lentils *(Moong Dhuli)*
3 cups Hot Tap Water (reduces cooking time)
10 ounce Frozen Chopped Spinach *(Palak)*–thawed
1 tablespoon Olive Oil *(Jaitoon Ka Tel)*
1 teaspoon Minced Ginger and Green Chili *(Adrak-Hari Mirch)*
½ teaspoon Turmeric Powder *(Haldi)*
1½ teaspoons Salt *(Namak)*

For Tempering:
2 tablespoons Olive Oil *(Jaitoon Ka Tel)*
pinch of Asafoetida *(Heeing)*
½ teaspoon Cumin Seeds *(Zeera)*
1 medium Onion *(Pyaz)*– finely chopped
1 big Clove Garlic *(Lehsun)*–grated
½ teaspoon Turmeric Powder *(Haldi)*
¼ teaspoon Red Chili Powder *(Lal Mirch)*
½ teaspoon Mango Powder *(Amchoor)*

For Garnish: 1 tablespoon chopped Cilantro *(Hara Dhaniya)*

Method:
Rinse the lentils 3-4 times in water, or until the water is clear. Then, soak in 3 cups of water for 15 minutes. Meanwhile, squeeze all the water content from the spinach, and set aside for later use.

In a medium pot, heat oil over low-medium heat. Add ginger-green chili, turmeric, salt, spinach, and 2 cups of water from the soaked lentils. Stir to mix everything well.

Increase the heat to medium-high, until water comes to a boil, then reduce the heat to low-medium. Cover and cook for 15 minutes, until the spinach changes color to one shade lighter, and is partially cooked.

Add lentils with the remaining 1 cup water, and mix again. Increase the heat to medium-high, until the soup comes to a boil.

Reduce the heat to low-medium. Cover and cook for 20 minutes, until lentils are soft, but not mushy, and spinach cooks through.

Check the seasoning, and add more as needed. If soup is too thick, add ½ cup hot water; then gently stir to bring it to the right consistency. Transfer the soup into a serving dish, and prepare the tempering.

For tempering: Heat oil in a small pan over medium heat, then add asafoetida, and let it sizzle. Add cumin seeds, and wait until they crackle.

Add onions, and sauté, for about 6-8 minutes, until golden brown. Add garlic, and stir-fry for a minute, until fragrant, then add turmeric, red chili powder, and mango powder.

Give a quick swirl, and pour the tempering over the soup. Garnish with cilantro, and serve hot Dal Palak with fresh roti, accompanied with vegetable yogurt sauce, onion relish, and roasted papadam.

Variations:
-Cook soup with 1 tablespoon fenugreek leaves for additional flavor.
-Substitute moong lentils with mixed lentils, then follow the recipe.
-Cook soup with garlic, onions and tomatoes, then add plain tempering.
-Add tomatoes to the tempering for additional sweet and tangy flavor.
-Substitute mango powder with lemon juice for some tang and freshness.

Dal Palak *(Lentil Spinach Soup)*

Sukhi Urad
(Tempered Dry Urad Lentils)

Sukhi Urad is *tempered dry urad lentils,* originating from the Punjab region in India. This dish is prepared from split urad lentils with onion and garlic tempering added on top. It is a spicy and delicious lentil dish, eaten with tava roti, onion relish, and yogurt sauce.

Serves 4
Ingredients:

Prep Time: 10 minutes
Cooking Time: 40 minutes
Inactive Time: 4 hours

1 cup Split Urad Lentils *(Urad Dhuli)*
3 cups, plus ½ cup Hot Tap Water
1 tablespoon Olive Oil *(Jaitoon Ka Tel)*
½ teaspoon Turmeric Powder *(Haldi)*
1 teaspoon Salt *(Namak)*

For Tempering:
2 tablespoons Olive Oil *(Jaitoon Ka Tel)*
pinch of Asafoetida *(Heeing)*
½ teaspoon Cumin Seeds *(Zeera)*
1 medium Onion *(Pyaz)*–chopped
1 big Clove Garlic *(Lehsun)*–grated
1 teaspoon Minced Ginger and Green Chili *(Adrak-Hari Mirch)*
1/8 teaspoon Turmeric Powder *(Haldi)*
Salt *(Namak)*–as needed
½ teaspoon Red Chili Powder *(Lal Mirch)*
2 tablespoons Lime Juice *(Neembu Rus)*

For Garnish:
½ Lime *(Neembu)*–quartered
1 tablespoon Chopped Cilantro *(Hara Dhaniya)*

Method:
Rinse the lentils 3-4 times in water, or until the water is clear, then soak them in 3 cups water for 4 hours. Soaked lentils cook faster, and don't get overcooked. Rinse again, then strain the lentils.

Spread them on a sheet pan, and cover with paper towel, then lightly pat them down several times, until all water is absorbed, leaving them dry.

Heat the oil over low-medium heat, in a wide non-stick skillet. Add turmeric, salt, and lentils along with ½ cup hot tap water, then stir to mix everything well.

Increase the heat to medium, and allow the water to boil. As it boils, some *foam*–*jhaag,* comes on top of the lentils; remove it with a spoon.

Reduce the heat to low. Cover and cook for 10 minutes, then gently stir. Partially cover, and cook for 10 more minutes. Stir once or twice to prevent burning, until most of the water has evaporated.

If lentils are not cooked, add 1 teaspoon water at a time, until it cooks and doesn't get mushy–the grains stay separate and *al dente.* Turn off the heat, and leave it covered for 5 minutes, to simmer in its own steam.

Check the seasoning, and add more as needed. Fluff the lentils with a fork, then transfer into a serving dish, and prepare the tempering.

For Tempering: Heat oil in a small pan over medium heat. Add asafoetida, and let it sizzle, then add cumin seeds, and allow them to crackle. Add onions, and sauté, for about 6-8 minutes, until golden brown. Add garlic, and ginger-green chili, then sauté for another minute.

Add turmeric, red chili powder, and salt–as needed, then give a quick swirl and pour over lentils in a circular motion. Squeeze some lime juice on top, and gently mix to incorporate all flavors.

Garnish with cilantro, and lime quarters. Serve hot Sukhi Urad with fresh roti, accompanied with onion relish, vegetable yogurt sauce, mint chutney, and papadam.

Sukhi Urad *(Tempered Dry Urad Lentils)*

Rajma Curry
(Red Kidney Beans Curry)

Rajma Curry is *red kidney beans curry*, originating from the Punjab region in India. It is prepared from dark red kidney beans, cooked in tomato and onion sauce. Rajma curry is mainly eaten with rice, but it tastes delicious with roti too. For this recipe, I have used canned kidney beans, as they cook faster, but you can also use raw beans to prepare this curry.

Serves 6
Ingredients:

Prep Time: 15 minutes
Cooking Time: 55 minutes

3 cans Dark Red Kidney Beans *(Rajma)*
2 tablespoons Olive Oil *(Jaitoon Ka Tel)*
½ teaspoon Cumin Seeds *(Zeera)*
1 big Onion *(Pyaz)*–finely chopped
pinch of Asafoetida *(Heeing)*
1 big Clove Garlic *(Lehsun)*–grated
1 tablespoon Minced Ginger and Green Chili *(Adrak-Hari Mirch)*
1 teaspoon Turmeric Powder *(Haldi)*
2 teaspoons Salt *(Namak)*
1 teaspoon Red Chili Powder *(Lal Mirch)*
2 teaspoons Coriander Powder *(Dhaniya)*
1 teaspoon Roasted Cumin Powder *(Bhuna Zeera)*
2 medium Tomatoes *(Timatar)*–finely chopped
½ cup Tomato Juice *(Timatar Rus)*
3 cups Hot Tap Water (reduces cooking time)
1 tablespoon Chopped Cilantro *(Hara Dhaniya)*

Method:

Open the cans and strain the kidney beans in a colander. Rinse them under running water, for 1-2 minutes, to remove all the preservatives and liquid. Set them aside for later use.

In a medium pot, heat the oil over medium heat, then add cumin seeds, and allow them to crackle. Add onions and sauté them, for about 6-8 minutes, until golden. Add asafoetida, and let it sizzle.

Reduce the heat to low-medium, and add garlic, ginger-green chili, and dry spices–turmeric, salt, red chili, coriander, and roasted cumin powder. Stir-fry for one minute, until fragrant.

Add tomatoes and tomato juice, then stir. Cover and cook, for about 10 minutes, until tomatoes are soft, and the oil separates. Add kidney beans and water, then stir to mix everything well.

Increase the heat to medium-high, and allow the curry to come to a boil. Reduce the heat back to low-medium, then cover and cook for 30 minutes, until the curry is thicker–the beans are softer, and a little mushy. Stir a few times in between to prevent burning.

Turn off the heat, and let the curry sit for 5 minutes covered, to allow the flavors to infuse together. Transfer the curry into a serving dish, and garnish with cilantro. Serve hot Rajma Curry with plain rice or roti, accompanied with onion relish, and sweet gourd yogurt sauce.

Variations:
-*Raw Kidney Beans*: Rinse and soak 2 cups raw kidney beans overnight, in 4 cups of hot tap water and 1 teaspoon of baking soda. Rinse the beans under running water to get rid of the soda water. Add 4 cups of fresh hot tap water, ½ teaspoon each of turmeric powder and ginger powder, plus 2 teaspoons salt, to the beans, and mix. Turn on the heat to medium-high, until water comes to a boil. Then, reduce the heat to low-medium; cover and cook for 60 minutes, until beans are tender, and cooked through. Follow the steps to prepare the curry as indicated above.

Rajma Curry *(Red Kidney Bean Curry)*

Masala Choley
(Spicy Chick Pea Curry)

Masala Choley is *spicy chick pea curry*, or *punjabi choley*; from Punjab region in India, and originated in Middle East. They are prepared from canned or raw chick peas–*kabuli chaney*, cooked in tomato and onion sauce. Here, I have used canned chick peas, as they cook faster.

Serves 6
Ingredients:

Prep Time: 20 minutes
Cooking Time: 1 hour 10 minutes

3 cans Chick Peas/Garbanzo Beans *(Choley)*
2 cups, plus ½ cup Hot Tap Water (reduces cooking time)
4 tablespoons Olive Oil *(Jaitoon Ka Tel)*
1 teaspoon Cumin Seeds *(Zeera)*
2 medium Onions *(Pyaz)*–minced
1 big Clove Garlic *(Lehsun)*–grated
1 teaspoon Minced Ginger and Green Chili *(Adrak-Hari Mirch)*
¼ teaspoon Turmeric Powder *(Haldi)*
1 teaspoon Red Chili Powder *(Lal Mirch)*
2 teaspoons Salt *(Namak)*–add more as needed
4 teaspoons Coriander Powder *(Dhaniya)*
2 teaspoons Roasted Cumin Powder *(Bhuna Zeera)*
2 teaspoons Mixed Spice *(Garam Masala)*–divided
1 big Tomato *(Timatar)*–pureed
¼ teaspoon Tamarind Paste *(Imli)*

For Garnish
1 medium Red Onion *(Lal Pyaz)* Rings–thinly sliced
1 teaspoon Lime Juice *(Neembu Rus)*, Pinch of Salt *(Namak)*
1 Lime *(Neembu)*–quartered

Method:
Strain the chick peas in a colander, then rinse them for 1-2 minutes under running water, until all the liquid and the preservatives are removed, which makes it hard to digest them.

Boil the chick peas in 2 cups water, for 5 minutes over medium heat. Then, reduce the heat to low-medium; cover and cook them for 10 more minutes, until tender.

Note: The canned chick peas are a little tough, so they need to be boiled, before adding to the sauce.

Heat the oil in a heavy base pot, over medium heat, then add the cumin seeds, and let them crackle. Add minced onions, and sauté, for 5 minutes, until lightly golden. Add garlic and ginger-green chili, then sauté for a minute, until fragrant.

Reduce the heat to low-medium, and add turmeric, red chili, salt, coriander, cumin, and 1 teaspoon mixed spice; then sauté for 30 seconds.

Add tomato puree and tamarind paste, then stir, until well mixed. Cover and cook, for 10 minutes, until a thick sauce has formed. Stir a few times.

Add chickpeas with the water they were boiled in, plus ½ cup extra water. Gently stir, then cover and cook, for another 30 minutes, until the curry has thickened–the chick peas are cooked, and the oil separates.

Add the remaining mixed spice, then gently stir again and turn off the heat. Keep it covered for a few minutes, to let the flavors infuse.

Make instant pickled onion rings garnish, by adding a pinch of salt, and lime juice, then mix and set aside for a few minutes.

Transfer the spicy curry into a serving dish, and garnish with lime, and the pickled onions.

Serve hot Masala Choley with bhatura, naan, kulcha, or rice accompanied with mint chutney, and boondi yogurt sauce.

Variations:
-Soak and rinse the raw chick peas, same as the raw red kidney beans. Then cook for 60 minutes until tender.

Masala Choley *(Spicy Chick Pea Curry)*

Masala Kaale Chaney
(Spicy Black Grams Curry)

Kaale Chaney, also known as *bengal grams*, are cooked in spices, and are called *spicy black grams*. They are prepared during religious festivals in India and are offered as Prasadam–*sacred food*, to Deities–*Indian Gods*. They are high in protein, and are one of the earliest cultivated legumes, mostly grown in the Indian subcontinent, Ethiopia, Mexico, and Iran. Bengal grams are green in color, when freshly grown–called *choliya*, and on drying, they turn into a dark brown/black color–called *kaale chaney*.

Serves 6

Ingredients:

Prep Time: 10 minutes
Cooking Time: 1 hour
Inactive time: 12 hours

2 cups Raw Black Grams *(Kaale Chaney)*
1 teaspoon Baking Soda
4 cups Hot Tap Water–for soaking
4 cups Hot Tap Water–for cooking (reduces cooking time)
4 tablespoons Olive Oil *(Jaitoon Ka Tel)*–divided
1 teaspoon Turmeric Powder *(Haldi)*–divided
1½ teaspoons Salt *(Namak)*–divided
pinch of Asafoetida *(Heeing)* *(optional)*
1 teaspoon Cumin Seeds *(Zeera)*
1 teaspoon Minced Ginger and Green Chili *(Adrak-Hari Mirch)*
1 teaspoon Roasted Cumin Powder *(Bhuna Zeera)*
1 teaspoon Red Chili Powder *(Lal Mirch)*
2 teaspoons Coriander Powder *(Dhaniya)*
1 teaspoon Mixed Spice *(Garam Masala)*
2 teaspoons Mango Powder *(Amchoor)*
1 tablespoon Chopped Cilantro *(Hara Dhaniya)*
½ Onion *(Pyaz)* Rings, pickled in salt, and lemon juice–for garnish

Method:

Rinse and soak the black grams in water and baking soda, overnight. Strain and rinse them again, then add 4 cups fresh hot water for cooking.

Heat 2 tablespoons of oil in a medium pot, over low-medium heat. Then, add ½ teaspoon turmeric, 1 teaspoon salt, and the black grams along with the fresh water; and mix.

Increase the heat to medium-high, until the water comes to a boil. Reduce the heat to low-medium, then cover and cook for 60 minutes, until water is reduced to about half a cup, and the grams are soft, and cooked through. Press one between your thumb and index finger to check.

If they are not cooked, add ½ cup of hot water, and cook for another 15 minutes, or until they are done.

For Spicy Gravy–*Masala:* Heat the remaining oil, in a small pan, over medium heat. Add asafoetida, and let it sizzle, then add cumin seeds, and allow them to crackle.

Reduce the heat to low, and add the remaining turmeric powder and salt; ginger-green chili, cumin powder, red chili, coriander, and mixed spice, then sauté for 30 seconds. Add the masala to the boiled grams, and mix well. Check the seasoning, and add more as needed.

Cover and simmer the black grams curry, for another 20 minutes, until it is thick. Stir a few times in between. Add the mango powder, and mix well, then leave it covered for 5 minutes, to let all flavors blend.

Transfer the curry into a serving dish, and garnish with cilantro, and pickled onion rings. Serve hot Masala Kaale Chaney with bhatura, kulcha or parantha, accompanied with potato yogurt sauce, mint chutney, and radish relish.

Variations: -Add 2 medium potatoes, peeled, quartered and boiled to the masala kaale chaney while cooking, for additional flavor.

Masala Kaale Chaney *(Spicy Black Grams Curry)*

Vegetable Curries and Snacks

I love vegetables, and can do so much with them, by using them in different ways, such as: making curries, snacks, condiments, beverages, and even use them for medicinal purposes. Vegetables are good for health, and vegetarians are healthy people. Some vegetables, such as: ginger and lemon, are used as spices, as well as for digestive purposes. My favorite vegetable curries are: Aloo Gobhi Masala, Aloo Methi Masala, Bhurma Karela, Baingan Bhurta, Bhurma Baingan, Kadhi Pakori, Khatta Meetha Kaddu, Malai Kofta, Masala Bhindi, Matar Paneer, Mooli Baingan, Palak Paneer, Rasa Pakori, and Sarson Ka Saag.

My favorite snacks are: Aloo Tikki, Sabzi Pakora, Kurkuree Hari Phali, Dhokla, Namkeen Sooji Halwa, Meetha Dalia, Bandgobhi Bonda, Neembu Cheelay, Vegetable Samosa, Pastry Crisps, Baked Namak Pare, and Shakarkandi Hash.

Aloo Gobhi Masala *(Spicy Potato Cauliflower Curry) Recipe on P80*

Aloo Gobhi Masala
(Spicy Potato Cauliflower Curry)

Aloo Gobhi is a North Indian *spicy potato cauliflower curry*, prepared from potatoes and cauliflower, cooked in onion and tomato sauce, and is eaten with plain tava roti, parantha, naan, bhatura or kulcha.

Serves 4
Ingredients:

Prep Time: 25 minutes
Cooking Time: 1 hour 10 minutes

3 tablespoons Olive Oil *(Jaitoon Ka Tel)*
½ teaspoon Cumin Seeds *(Zeera)*
1 medium Onion *(Pyaz)*–finely chopped
1 big Clove Garlic *(Lehsun)*–grated
1 teaspoon Minced Ginger and Green Chili *(Adrak-Hari Mirch)*
½ teaspoon Turmeric Powder *(Haldi)*
3 teaspoons Coriander Powder *(Dhaniya)*
½ teaspoon Red Chili Powder *(Lal Mirch)*
1 teaspoon Roasted Cumin Powder *(Bhuna Zeera)*
1 teaspoon Salt *(Namak)*
2 medium Tomatoes *(Timatar)*–finely chopped
1 small head of Cauliflower *(Gobhi)*–cut into florets
2 medium Potatoes *(Aloo)*–peeled and diced
1 teaspoon Mango Powder *(Amchoor)*
½ teaspoon Mixed Spice *(Garam Masala)*
2 tablespoons Chopped Cilantro *(Hara Dhaniya)*

Method:

Heat oil in a karahi or a wok over medium heat, then add cumin seeds, and allow them to crackle. Add onions and sauté, for 6-8 minutes, until golden, then add garlic and sauté for a minute, until fragrant.

Reduce the heat to low-medium, and add ginger-green chili, turmeric, coriander, red chili, cumin powder, and salt, then cook for 1 minute.

Add tomatoes, then mix; cover, and cook for 5-7 minutes, until they are soft, mushy, and form a sauce. Add cauliflower and potatoes, then mix well to coat them with the tomato sauce.

Cover and cook for 15 minutes, until vegetables are slightly tender. Partially cover, and cook for 35 minutes, until they cook through, and most of the moisture evaporates. Gently stir occasionally.

Add mango powder, and mixed spice, then gently mix to incorporate everything well. Transfer the curry into a serving dish, and garnish with cilantro. Serve hot Aloo Gobhi Masala with fresh roti, parantha, naan, or kulcha, accompanied with boondi yogurt sauce, and mint chutney.

Aloo Methi Masala
(Spicy Potato Fenugreek Curry)

Aloo Methi Masala is a north Indian dry *spicy potato fenugreek curry*, prepared from fresh or dry fenugreek leaves and potatoes, and is eaten with plain roti, parantha, bhatura, naan, or kulcha. I have used dry fenugreek leaves for this recipe.

Serves 4

Ingredients:

Prep Time: 20 minutes
Cooking Time: 1 hour

1 cup Dry Fenugreek Leaves *(Kasoori Methi)*
2 cups, plus 3 tablespoons Water
6 medium Potatoes *(Aloo)* washed, cubed with skin–soaked in water
4 tablespoons Olive Oil *(Jaitoon Ka Tel)*
pinch of Asafoetida *(Heeing)*
1 teaspoon Cumin Seeds *(Zeera)*
1 medium Onion *(Pyaz)*–finely chopped
1 big Clove Garlic *(Lehsun)*–grated
1 teaspoon Minced Ginger and Green Chili *(Adrak-Hari Mirch)*
1 teaspoon Turmeric Powder *(Haldi)*
2 teaspoons Coriander Powder *(Dhaniya)*
½ teaspoon Red Chili Powder *(Lal Mirch)*
1½ teaspoons Salt *(Namak)*
1 teaspoon Roasted Cumin Powder *(Bhuna Zeera)*
½ teaspoon Mixed Spice *(Garam Masala)*
1 teaspoon Mango Powder *(Amchoor)*

Method:
Soak the dry fenugreek leaves in 2 cups water, for 15 minutes, until rehydrated and sand settles to the bottom. Then, carefully spoon them out from the top, and set aside in a bowl for later use.

Heat the oil in a wok, over medium heat. Add asafoetida, and let it sizzle, then add cumin seeds, and allow them to crackle. Add onions, and sauté them, for 5 minutes, until translucent.

Reduce the heat to low-medium, then add garlic, ginger-green chili, turmeric, coriander, red chili powder, salt, cumin powder, and mixed spice. Stir-fry for a minute, until aromatic, and the oil separates.

Add fenugreek leaves, and mix well. Then, add 3 tablespoons water to make some steam, and mix again. Cover, and cook, for 3 minutes, until the leaves are soft, and the oil separates. Stir a few times in between.

Strain the potatoes, and add them to the fenugreek leaves, then mix well. Cover and cook, for 15 minutes over low-medium heat, until potatoes are soft, but not mushy, and hold their shape.

Uncover, and cook, for another 30 minutes, until most of the moisture evaporates, and the oil separates. Check every 5 minutes to prevent burning. Add the mango powder, and gently mix.

Leave it covered for a few minutes, allowing all flavors to infuse together. Then, transfer the curry into a serving dish. Serve hot Aloo Methi Masala with roti or parantha, accompanied with vegetable raita and mint chutney

Variations:
-Substitute potatoes and dry fenugreek with mushrooms and fresh fenugreek. Cook as in recipe above, then add ¼ cup heavy cream. Cook for 5 more minutes, then serve. It is creamy and delicious.

-Add ½ cup frozen, and thawed *spinach* to the dish for additional flavor.
-Substitute mango powder with *sautéed tomatoes*, or *lemon juice*, then toss, to add some tang and fresh flavor to the dish.

Bhurma Karela
(Stuffed Bitter Gourd)

Bhurma Karela is a dry spicy north Indian side dish, called *stuffed bitter gourd*. It is prepared from bitter gourd, stuffed with a spicy mix, then cooked in little oil. Karela also has medicinal qualities, especially its juice, which is bitter, but good for health.

Serves 2
Ingredients:

Prep Time: 10 minutes
Cooking Time: 55 minutes
Inactive Time: 15 minutes

4 Bitter Gourds *(Karela)*
4 tablespoons Olive Oil *(Jaitoon Ka Tel)*–divided
1½ teaspoons Salt *(Namak)*–divided
¼ teaspoon Turmeric Powder *(Haldi)*
¼ teaspoon Red Chili Powder *(Lal Mirch)*
1 teaspoon Coriander Powder *(Dhaniya)*
1 teaspoon Mango Powder *(Amchoor)*
1 teaspoon Fennel Seeds *(Saunf)*
½ teaspoon Roasted Cumin Powder *(Bhuna Zeera)*
¼ teaspoon Ginger Powder *(Pisa Adrak)*
2 teaspoons Water
1 Onion *(Pyaz)*–cut into rings
1 tablespoon Chopped Cilantro *(Hara Dhaniya)*

Method:

First, scrape off the hard rough skin of all the bitter gourds, then rub 1 teaspoon salt on them generously and evenly. Set them aside, for 15 minutes, in a colander with a bowl placed underneath, to drain and get rid of most of their bitter juice.

Meanwhile, combine turmeric, red chili powder, coriander, remaining salt; mango powder, fennel seeds, cumin powder, ginger, and water, then mix well, and set aside to use later for stuffing the gourds.

Rinse all the gourds under running water, while gently rubbing them to remove their bitterness, and the salt. Then, gently squeeze them, to remove all the water content, and dry them with a paper towel.

Cut a slit on one side of each gourd, like a pocket, from top to bottom. Then, stuff them with the spice mix, equally distributing it between them. Heat 2 tablespoons of oil in a non-stick pan, over low-medium heat, and place the stuffed bitter gourds, carefully, slit side up.

Cover and cook them for 20 minutes. Then, uncover and cook for another 20 minutes, until charred, and crispy on all sides. Turn them every 5 minutes, so they cook evenly.

Meanwhile, in another non-stick pan, heat the remaining 2 tablespoons of oil, over medium heat, and sauté onion rings, for 5-6 minutes, until lightly golden, and caramelized, then sprinkle some salt on top.

For Serving: Spread the caramelized onion rings, on a serving platter like a bed, then place the stuffed bitter gourds on top.

Sprinkle cilantro, and serve hot Bhurma Karela, as a side dish with dal tadka, plain roti, or parantha. The caramelized onions are sweet and salty, and a delicious garnish for spicy, crispy and charred bhurma karelas.

Variations:
-*For Stuffing:* Sauté a chopped onion, in little oil, until translucent. Remove from heat, and mix in the dry spices. Stuff gourds with the onion mix, then follow the remaining steps as in the recipe above.

-For *Bitter Gourd Curry*–*Karela Bhujia:* Once the gourds are scraped, salted and rinsed, slice them and set aside. Sauté a chopped onion, add spices, then stir-fry for a minute. Add gourd slices, and mix; cover and cook, for 25 minutes, until they are golden, crispy, and cooked through.

Bhurma Karela *(Stuffed Bitter Gourd)*

Baingan Bhurta
(Eggplant Baba Ganoush)

Baingan Bhurta is like *eggplant baba ganoush*–an Arabic dish; and it originates from the Punjab region in India. It is prepared from charcoal roasted eggplants, to infuse a smoky flavor to the dish. My mother used to leave 4-5 medium eggplants, in the lower part of the charcoal burner, where the heat was low, and let them roast, until the other cooking was done. These can also be roasted on a gas burner over a low flame, or on a hot griddle on an electric stovetop, or broiled at 500 degree F.

Serves 4
Ingredients:

Prep Time: 35 minutes
Cooking Time: 55 minutes

1 medium Firm Eggplant *(Baingan)*
4 tablespoons Olive Oil *(Jaitoon Ka Tel)*
pinch of Asafoetida *(Heeing)* (optional)
½ teaspoon Cumin Seeds *(Zeera)*
1 big Onion *(Pyaz)*–finely chopped
1 big Clove Garlic *(Lehsun)*–grated
1 teaspoon Minced Ginger and Green Chili *(Adrak-Hari Mirch)*
1 big Tomato *(Timatar)*–finely chopped
¼ cup Tomato Juice *(Timatar Rus)*
½ teaspoon Turmeric Powder *(Haldi)*
½ teaspoon Salt *(Namak)*–add more as needed
½ teaspoon Red Chili Powder *(Lal Mirch)*
2 teaspoons Coriander Powder *(Dhaniya)*
½ teaspoon Roasted Cumin Powder *(Bhuna Zeera)*
½ teaspoon Mixed Spice *(Garam Masala)*
1 sprig of Mint *(Podina)*–for garnish

Method:
Wash and pat dry the eggplant, then prick twice with a fork, before grilling. Pricking prevents it from bursting with hot steam, which can be dangerous, when turning the eggplant.

Grill the eggplant on a hot griddle, over medium heat, for 15-20 minutes, or until the skin is charred and crumbly. At this point, the steam starts to release, and the water seeps out. Use kitchen tongs to turn the eggplant, every 2-3 minutes to allow even charring on all sides.

Turn off the heat, and transfer the charred eggplant, into a bowl, then cover with a plastic wrap, for about 10 minutes. Covering helps the skin to loosen, and come off easily. Peel off the skin by hand, then mash the eggplant pulp with a fork, into a puree, and set aside in the same bowl, for later use.

In a medium skillet, heat the oil over medium heat. Add asafoetida, and let it sizzle, then add the cumin seeds, and allow them to crackle. Add the onions, and sauté, for about 6-8 minutes, until golden brown.

Add garlic, and ginger-green chili, then stir-fry for a minute, until fragrant. Add tomatoes, tomato juice, turmeric, salt, red chili, coriander, cumin, and mixed spice; then mix. Cover and cook for about 5-7 minutes, until a smooth sauce forms, and the oil separates. Stir in between.

Reduce the heat to low-medium, and add the eggplant puree to the sauce, then mix well. Cover, and cook for 30 minutes, until the oil separates–the puree cooks through, and it smells roasted. Stir occasionally.

Transfer the curry into a serving dish, and garnish with mint. Serve hot Baingan Bhurta with fresh roti, parantha, bhatura, naan or kulcha, accompanied with vegetable raita, onion relish, and roasted papadam.

Variations:
-Substitute tomato, and tomato juice, with ½ cup of plain yogurt, and 1 tablespoon lemon juice, then mix and serve. My mother used to make baingan bhurta this way, when I first tasted it, and it was delicious!

-Substitute roasted eggplant with peeled and cubed eggplant. Then, cook it with onions, garlic, and spices; without the tomatoes, until soft. Follow the remaining steps as in recipe above.

Baingan Parmesan
(Eggplant Parmesan)

Eggplant Parmesan is my twist on the original recipe, without adding the parmesan cheese. It is creamy, light, delicious, and full of flavor.

Serves 2
Ingredients:

Prep Time: 20 minutes
Cooking Time: 55 minutes

1 medium Eggplant *(Baingan)*–sliced into 1/8 inch thick rounds
4 tablespoons Olive Oil *(Jaitoon Ka Tel)*–divided
2 medium Onions *(Pyaz)*–finely chopped
1 big Clove Garlic *(Lehsun)*–grated
½ teaspoon Turmeric Powder *(Haldi)*
½ teaspoon Ginger Powder *(Pisa Adrak)*
2 teaspoons Coriander Powder *(Dhaniya)*
1 teaspoon Salt *(Namak)*–add more as needed
½ teaspoon Red Chili Powder *(Lal Mirch)*
1½ teaspoons Roasted Cumin Powder *(Bhuna Zeera)*
1½ cups Vegetable Juice *(Subzi Rus)*
4 mini Sweet Peppers *(Choti Shimla Mirch)*–deseeded and julienned
1½ cups Grated Mozzarella Cheese
1 teaspoon Chopped Cilantro *(Hara Dhaniya)*–for garnish

Method:
Heat a grill pan over medium heat, then lightly brush the eggplant slices with oil. Grill 4 slices at a time, for 2-3 minutes on each side, pressing them down with a spatula, until golden brown and cooked through. Check by inserting a toothpick.

Transfer the grilled slices on to a paper towel, to drain excess oil, then sprinkle some salt on top. Repeat and grill the remaining slices.

Heat the remaining oil in a non-stick pan over medium heat. Add onions and sauté, for about 5 minutes, until lightly golden. Add garlic, and sauté, for 30 seconds.

Reduce the heat to low-medium, then add the dry spices–turmeric, ginger, coriander, salt, red chili, and cumin powder. Sauté for a minute, then add the vegetable juice, and mix. Cook for 8-10 minutes, over medium heat, until a thick sauce forms.

Add the sweet peppers, then mix and cook, for another 2-3 minutes, until they are tender but still crunchy, and the oil separates.

In a medium pregreased oven dish, spoon **First** layer of half the sauce, to cover its base evenly. Spread grilled eggplant slices for the **Second** layer. For the **Third** layer–spread half the mozzarella cheese evenly. For the **Fourth** layer–spread the remaining eggplant slices.

For the **Fifth** layer–spread the remaining sauce, and for **Sixth** and **final** layer spread an even layer of the remaining cheese.

Place the oven rack 10 inch below the broiler, then turn on the broiler (500 degrees F). Place the oven dish under it, and broil for 10 minutes, until cheese is bubbly and golden. Turn off the broiler, and leave in the dish for 2 more minutes. Remove and garnish with cilantro and serve hot Baingan Parmesan with plain pasta.

Variations:
-Substitute the vegetable sauce with white sauce, and broil.
-Substitute eggplant with cauliflower and mushrooms, then broil.
-Substitute eggplant with boiled potato slices, and vegetable sauce with white sauce. Top it with cheese, and bread crumbs, then broil.

Baingan Parmesan *(Eggplant Parmesan)*

Bhurma Baingan
(Stuffed Baby Eggplant)

Bhurma Baingan are *baby eggplants*, stuffed with a mix of Indian spices, and are eaten with roti, plain parantha, or kulcha.

Serves 4
Ingredients:
For Stuffing:

Prep Time: 15 minutes
Cooking Time: 30 minutes

½ teaspoon Turmeric Powder *(Haldi)*
½ teaspoon Red Chili Powder *(Lal Mirch)*
½ teaspoon Salt *(Namak)*
3 teaspoons Coriander Powder *(Dhaniya)*
½ teaspoon Ginger Powder *(Pisa Adrak)*
½ teaspoon Roasted Cumin Powder *(Bhuna Zeera)*
½ teaspoon Mango Powder *(Amchoor)*
½ teaspoon Fennel Seeds *(Saunf)*
1 teaspoon Water

Also Needed:
8 Baby Eggplants *(Chote Baingan)*
3 tablespoons Olive Oil *(Jaitoon Ka Tel)*
Fresh Chopped Cilantro, and 8 Toothpicks *(Optional)*

Method:
In a small bowl, combine the dry spices–turmeric, red chili, salt, coriander, ginger, cumin, mango powder, and fennel seeds. Mix well. Adjust the spices according to your taste. Add a little water to the spices, and mix well to form a thick paste, making it easy to stuff the baby eggplants. Set aside the paste for later use.

Wash and pat dry the baby eggplants, then hold each one by the stem, and place it flat on its side, on a cutting board. Carefully run a knife from just below the stem, making a slit lengthwise to the bottom end, cutting it into two halves, while keeping it attached to the stem.

Turn it halfway, and cut another slit in the same way, to make a cross slit, leaving the stems on, to hold and turn them while cooking.

Gently open the slit a little, and spoon the spice mix in each eggplant, in a single layer, as evenly as possible, until all are stuffed. Stick a toothpick *(optional)* in each eggplant, to prevent it from breaking while cooking.

Heat 3 tablespoons of oil, in a non-stick skillet, over medium heat. Place the stuffed eggplants, slit side facing in, and stem side facing out, arranged in a circle.

Cover and cook, for 20 minutes, then uncover and cook, for another 10 minutes, over low-medium heat, until crispy on all sides, and cooked through. Use kitchen tongs to turn eggplant sides every 5 minutes, for even cooking; then remove the toothpicks before serving.

Transfer the Bhurma Baingan on to a serving platter. Garnish with chopped cilantro, and serve hot with fresh roti, naan, or parantha, accompanied with cucumber raita, mint chutney, tomato chutney, and roasted papadam.

Variations:
-Scoop out the cooked eggplant pulp and spices with a spoon; mix in some ketchup, then spread on a garlic buttered baguette slice, to make a *crostini*. Top it with grated mozzarella cheese, and broil.

-Sauté 1 onion's rings, until lightly golden and caramelized, then sprinkle some salt on top. Spread them on to a serving platter, then place the stuffed baby eggplants on top, and serve. It tastes delicious!

Bhurma Baingan *(Stuffed Baby Eggplant)*

Kadhi Pakori
(Gram Flour Dumplings Curry)

Kadhi Pakori is *gram flour dumplings curry*, from the Gujarat region in western India. It is prepared from yogurt, and gram flour with a unique tangy flavor, and is eaten with plain rice or roti. Kadhi is more delicious when eaten the next day, as leftovers.

Serves 4
Ingredients:
For Dumplings: Makes 18

Prep Time: 20 minutes
Cooking Time: 1 hour 30 minutes

1 cup Gram Flour/Chick Pea Flour *(Besan)*
¼ Onion *(Pyaz)*–finely chopped
1 teaspoon Minced Ginger and Green Chili *(Adrak-Hari Mirch)*
2 tablespoons Chopped Cilantro *(Hara Dhaniya)*–divided
½ teaspoon Red Chili Powder *(Lal Mirch)*
½ teaspoon Salt *(Namak)*
pinch of Baking Soda
¼ cup, plus ½ cup Water
1 cup Vegetable Oil–for frying

For Curry
2 cups Plain Yogurt *(Dahi)*
¼ cup Gram Flour/Chick Pea Flour *(Besan)*
½ teaspoon Turmeric Powder *(Haldi)*
½ teaspoon Red Chili Powder *(Lal Mirch)*
1 teaspoon Salt *(Namak)*–add more as needed
2 tablespoons Olive Oil *(Jaitoon Ka Tel)*
½ teaspoon Cumin Seeds *(Zeera)*
5 cups, plus ¼ cup Water
2 tablespoons Dry Fenugreek Leaves *(Kasoori Methi)*

For Tempering
2 tablespoons Olive Oil *(Jaitoon Ka Tel)*
pinch of Asafoetida *(Heeing)*
1 teaspoon Mustard Seeds *(Rai)*
½ teaspoon Turmeric Powder *(Haldi)*
½ teaspoon Red Chili Powder *(Lal Mirch)*

Method:

For *Gram Flour Dumplings*–Besan Pakori; combine gram flour, onion, ginger-green chili, 1 tablespoon cilantro, red chili powder, salt, and baking soda in a bowl. Then add ¼ cup water, a little at a time, to make a smooth thick batter. Whip it to make light and fluffy dumplings. If it is too thick, add a little more water, and whip again.

Heat the oil in a karahi or a wok, over medium heat for a minute. Check the oil by dropping a little batter in it, which should sizzle and rise to the top in 30 seconds, and not turn brown.

Scoop 1 teaspoon of batter, and drop in the hot oil; 6-8 at a time, allowing them to have enough room to expand, and cook evenly. They will puff up like a ball. Then, reduce the heat to low-medium.

Fry for about 2-3 minutes, until lightly golden on all sides, then remove with a slotted spoon on to a paper towel, to drain excess oil. Repeat, until all the batter is finished. Set them aside to cool, and use later.

Add the remaining ½ cup water to the empty batter bowl, and whisk it to collect the last bits of the batter. Set aside to use later in the curry.

For Curry–Kadhi: Combine yogurt, gram flour, turmeric, red chili powder, and salt in a large bowl. Whisk to break up any lumps, until smooth. Slowly incorporate water, one cup at a time, plus the batter water saved earlier, until a smooth watery consistency mix is formed. Set aside the yogurt mix for 5 minutes.

Heat the oil in a medium heavy base pot, over medium-high heat. Then, add the cumin seeds, and allow them to crackle.

Remove the pot from heat, and stir in the yogurt mix. Keep stirring constantly, to prevent it from curdling. Bring the pot back on heat, and continue stirring, for 8-10 minutes, until the curry comes to a boil.

Reduce the heat to low-medium, then partially cover, and cook for 45 minutes, or until the curry begins to thicken. Stir every 5 minutes, to prevent burning.

Meanwhile, soak the dry fenugreek leaves in ¼ cup water, and leave for 10 minutes, until the sand settles to the bottom. Then, spoon out the leaves from the top, and set them aside in a bowl.

Add dumplings, and fenugreek leaves, to the curry, then gently stir. Partially cover, and cook for 20 minutes, over low-medium heat, until the dumplings are soft; the curry begins to bubble; it thickens enough to coat the back of a spoon, and the aroma of fenugreek fills the room.

Turn off the heat, and leave it covered for 5 minutes. Carefully spoon out the dumplings, in to a serving dish, then pour the curry on top, and prepare the tempering.

For Tempering: Heat the oil in a small pan, over medium heat. Add asafoetida, and let it sizzle, then add mustard seeds, and allow them to crackle. Add turmeric, and red chili powder, then give it a quick swirl and pour the tempering over the curry, in a circular motion.

Cover it for 5 more minutes, allowing all the flavors to infuse together. Garnish with remaining cilantro, and serve hot Kadhi Pakori with plain basmati rice or fresh roti, and roasted papadam.

Variations:
-Serve just dumplings as snack, with tamarind and mint chutney.

-Soak the dumplings in yogurt sauce, with a dash of salt, cumin powder, and red chili powder, then serve chilled.

-Substitute onions with fresh fenugreek leaves, for the dumplings batter, then mix and fry the dumplings.

-Substitute dumplings with *Boondi*–*fried gram flour puffs*, and add to the curry, just before adding the tempering. Cover and leave the curry for 10 minutes, until boondi is soft, then add the tempering.

Kadhi Pakori *(Gram flour Dumplings Curry)*

Khatta Meetha Kaddu
(Tangy Sweet Pumpkin)

Khatta Meetha Kaddu is a delicious, *tangy sweet pumpkin* dish from north India. It is prepared from cheese pumpkin, sugar, and tamarind chutney, and is eaten with parantha, bhatura, or tava roti.

Serves 4
Ingredients:

Prep Time: 30 minutes
Cooking Time: 50 minutes

1½ pounds Cheese Pumpkin *(Kaddu)*
2 tablespoons dry Fenugreek Leaves *(Kasoori Methi)*
½ cup Water
¼ cup Olive Oil *(Jaitoon Ka Tel)*
pinch of Asafoetida *(Heeing)*
½ teaspoon Cumin Seeds *(Zeera)*
½ teaspoon Turmeric Powder *(Haldi)*
1 teaspoon Salt *(Namak)*–add more as needed
2 teaspoons Coriander Powder *(Dhaniya)*
½ teaspoon Red Chili Powder *(Lal Mirch)*
½ teaspoon Roasted Cumin Powder *(Bhuna Zeera)*
½ teaspoon Mixed Spice *(Garam Masala)*
1 teaspoon Minced Ginger and Green Chili *(Adrak-Hari Mirch)*
2 medium Tomatoes *(Timatar)*–finely chopped
1/8 cup Sugar *(Chini)*
3 tablespoons Tamarind Chutney *(Imli Ki Chutney)* Refer to Recipe on P27
1 tablespoon Chopped Cilantro *(Hara Dhaniya)*

Method:
Scoop out the fibers and the seeds from the center of the pumpkin, then peel it and cut into 1 inch cubes. Rinse them in a colander, then shake to remove all water, and set aside.

Soak the dry fenugreek leaves, in ½ cup water, for 10 minutes, until they rehydrate, and all the sand settles to the bottom. Then, carefully spoon out the leaves from top, and set them aside in a bowl.

Heat oil in a wok, over medium heat, then add asafoetida, and let it sizzle. Add cumin seeds, and allow them to crackle. Reduce the heat to low-medium, and add turmeric, salt, coriander, red chili, cumin powder, and mixed spice; then stir-fry for 30 seconds, until aromatic.

Add ginger-green chili, and tomatoes, then mix and cook, for 5-7 minutes, until they are soft, and form a thick sauce. Add fenugreek leaves, and mix again. Then, cover and cook for 5 minutes, until they are soft and fragrant.

Add the pumpkin cubes; then mix to coat them well with the tomato sauce. Cover and cook, for 10-15 minutes, until they are soft. Check a few times occasionally.

Add sugar, then gently mix. Uncover, and cook for another 15 minutes, over low-medium heat, until most of the moisture evaporates; since added sugar releases water.

By now, the pumpkin should be cooked through, still holding its shape; leaving the edges of the wok, and the oil separating.

Add the tamarind chutney and gently fold into the curry, to prevent the pumpkin from becoming mushy. Simmer uncovered for 5 minutes, until all the flavors come together.

Garnish with cilantro, and serve hot Khatta Meetha Kaddu with fresh roti, parantha, bhatura, or naan, accompanied with boondi yogurt sauce, and mint chutney.

Khatta Meetha Kaddu *(Tangy Sweet Pumpkin)*

Malai Kofta
(Vegetable Dumplings Curry)

Malai Kofta is one of the sophisticated *vegetable dumplings curry*. It is prepared from vegetable dumplings–*kofta pakori*, cooked in an onion-tomato gravy, with added cream on top. For this recipe, I have used only one vegetable to prepare the dumplings, keeping the dish lighter, but you can always use mixed vegetables to prepare them.

Serves 6
Ingredients:
For Dumplings: Makes 18

Prep Time: 20 minutes
Cooking Time: 1 hour 25 minutes
Inactive Time: 15 minutes

1 small Bottle Gourd *(Ghiya)*–peeled, and grated
1 medium Onion *(Pyaz)*–grated
½ teaspoon Minced Ginger and Green Chili *(Adrak-Hari Mirch)*
1 teaspoon Salt *(Namak)*
½ teaspoon Red Chili Powder *(Lal Mirch)*
6 heaped tablespoons Gram Flour *(Besan)*
¼ teaspoon Baking Soda
1 cup Vegetable Oil–for frying

For Gravy:
2 tablespoons Olive Oil *(Jaitoon Ka Tel)*
1 big Onion *(Pyaz)*–finely chopped
1 big Clove Garlic *(Lehsun)*–grated
1 teaspoon Minced Ginger and Green Chili *(Adrak-Hari Mirch)*
½ teaspoon Turmeric Powder *(Haldi)*
1 teaspoon Salt *(Namak)*
2 teaspoons Coriander Powder *(Dhaniya)*
½ teaspoon Red Chili Powder *(Lal Mirch)*
½ teaspoon Roasted Cumin Powder *(Bhuna Zeera)*
½ teaspoon Mixed Spice *(Garam Masala)*
2 big Tomatoes *(Timatar)*–finely chopped
½ cup Tomato Juice *(Timatar Rus)*
2 cups Hot Tap Water (reduces cooking time)
¼ cup Heavy Cream
1 tablespoon Chopped Cilantro *(Hara Dhaniya)*

Method:
For *Vegetable Dumplings*–*Kofta Pakori;* combine the grated bottle gourd and onions in a medium bowl, then squeeze to remove all their water content. Save the water to use later in preparing the gravy.

Add ginger-green chili, salt, red chili powder, gram flour, and baking soda, to the vegetables, then mix well to make a thick batter for the dumplings. If the batter is too thin, add more flour to thicken it.

Heat the oil in a wok, over medium heat. Check the oil by dropping a little batter in it, which should sizzle and rise to the top in 30 seconds, and not turn brown.

Take some batter with a small ice cream scoop, or a regular spoon, and carefully slide it into the hot oil from the side, to prevent the oil from splashing. Add 5 more scoops to make a batch of 6 dumplings.

Wait for 1 minute, then flip them over, to fry for 1 more minute, until golden brown on all sides. Reduce the heat to low-medium, then remove dumplings with a slotted spoon, on to a paper towel, to drain excess oil.

Repeat and fry the remaining dumplings, until the batter is finished, then set them aside to use later.

Note: The spices in the batter may release some moisture, making it soggy, so add a little more flour, then mix and fry the dumplings.

For Gravy: Heat oil in a medium saucepan, over medium heat, then add onions, and sauté for 6-8 minutes, until golden. Add garlic, and ginger-green chili, then sauté for another minute, until fragrant.

Add the dry spices–turmeric, salt, coriander, red chili, cumin powder, and mixed spice, then stir-fry for a minute, until aromatic. Add the tomatoes, and tomato juice, then mix and continue to cook, for 10 minutes, until a chunky sauce forms.

Turn off the heat, and allow it to cool for 15 minutes. Then, puree the chunky sauce in an electric blender, until smooth. Transfer the sauce back, into the same pan, then turn on the heat to low-medium, and cook for about 4-5 minutes, until bubbly, and the oil separates.

Add the vegetable water saved earlier, plus 2 cups more water to the sauce, and mix. Check the seasoning, and add more as needed.

Increase the heat, to medium-high, and let the curry come to a boil. Then reduce the heat, to low-medium, and add the dumplings. Stir gently, then cover and cook for 15 minutes, until the dumplings plump up and are double in size, and the gravy begins to thicken.

Reduce the heat further to low, then partially cover, and cook for 10 minutes, until gravy is thick enough to coat the dumplings. Turn off the heat, and leave it covered for 5 minutes until all flavors infuse together.

Gently spoon out the dumplings, into a serving dish, without breaking them. Then, mix the cream in to the gravy and slowly pour it over the dumplings, covering them evenly.

Garnish with cilantro, and serve hot Malai Kofta with naan, or bhatura, accompanied with tomato chutney, and onion relish.

Variations:
-Substitute bottle gourd with chinese okra *(silk squash)*, grated cabbage, or mixed vegetables, then follow the remaining steps as in the recipe to make dumplings.

-Substitute heavy cream with 1 tablespoon of unsalted butter for a lighter dish.
-Serve just dumplings as a snack, with tamarind and mint chutney.

-Substitute tomato juice with vegetable juice in the gravy for extra flavor.
-Substitute vegetable dumplings with *cottage cheese dumplings (P102)*, and follow the remaining steps as in the recipe above to prepare the curry.

Masala Bhindi
(Spicy Okra Curry)

Masala Bhindi is *spicy okra curry* prepared from sliced okra, stir-fried in a blend of spices, onions, and tomatoes.

Serves 4
Ingredients:

Prep Time: 25 minutes
Cooking Time: 50 minutes

1 pound Okra *(Bhindi)*
4 tablespoons Olive Oil *(Jaitoon Ka Tel)*
pinch of Asafoetida *(Heeing)*
¼ teaspoon Carom Seeds *(Ajwain)*
1 big Onion *(Pyaz)*–chopped
1 big Clove Garlic *(Lehsun)*–grated
1 teaspoon Turmeric Powder *(Haldi)*
2 teaspoons Coriander Powder *(Dhaniya)*
1 teaspoon Salt *(Namak)*
1 teaspoon Red Chili Powder *(Lal Mirch)*
1 teaspoon Roasted Cumin Powder *(Bhuna Zeera)*
½ teaspoon Minced Ginger and Green Chili *(Adrak-Hari Mirch)*
2 medium Tomatoes *(Timatar)*–chopped

Method:

Wash the okras, then spread them on a sheet pan, and pat dry completely with a paper towel. Any moisture remaining will make the okras slimy to touch, and will release more moisture, while cooking. Thus, okra is washed *before* cutting, and not after.

Trim both ends of each okra, then slice it length-ways into two halves. Further, cut each half into two–across the width, to make 4 pieces. Repeat, until all okras are sliced, then set them aside.

Heat the oil over medium heat, in a non-stick wok, and wait for a minute, then carefully add half the okras, and stir-fry, for 5 minutes, until tender, but still maintaining their shape. Reduce the heat to low, then remove the okras with a slotted spoon, and set aside in a bowl.

Repeat and stir-fry the remaining okras, then remove and set aside, leaving the excess oil in the wok. Add asafoetida and let it sizzle; then add carom seeds, and allow them to crackle.

Add the onions and sauté for 5 minutes, over medium heat, until translucent. Add garlic and sauté for another minute. Reduce the heat to low-medium, then add the dry spices; turmeric, coriander, salt, red chili powder, and cumin powder. Then, sauté for 1 minute.

Increase the heat to medium-low, then add ginger-green chili, and tomatoes; and sauté for 5 minutes, until the tomatoes are soft, but still hold their shape. Add the okra and cook uncovered, for 25 minutes, until it cooks through; most of the moisture evaporates, and everything incorporates. Check and turn often. Transfer it into a serving dish.

Serve hot Masala Bhindi with fresh roti, parantha, naan, or bhatura, accompanied with tomato chutney, and onion relish.

Note: Carom Seeds–*ajwain*, are highly fragrant with a lemony flavor. They smell and taste like thyme, but are stronger, so use only a little. They bring a nice aroma to the dish, and have many medicinal qualities.

Variations:
-Make *Stuffed Okra*–*Bhurma Bhindi,* by making a slit on one side like a pocket, then stuff the dry spice mix. Stir-fry okra in oil over medium heat, until soft, crispy and cooked through.

-Make *Okra Taco* by stuffing the spicy okra in the flour tortilla, then top it with mint chutney for extra tang and spice.

-Make *Okra Fritters*, by coating sliced okra with gram flour or white flour batter with seasoning to taste, then deep fry, until crispy golden.

Matar Paneer
(Peas Cottage Cheese Curry)

Matar Paneer is a rich, creamy *peas cottage cheese curry*, prepared from green peas and cottage cheese, cooked in tomato gravy. For this recipe, I have used low-fat milk, to prepare the cheese–keeping the dish lighter.

Serves 6

Prep Time: 5 hours

Ingredients:

Cooking Time: 1 hour 15 minutes

10 ounce block of Fresh Cottage Cheese *(Paneer) Refer to Recipe on P111*
4 tablespoons Olive Oil *(Jaitoon Ka Tel)*–divided
1 big Onion *(Pyaz)*–chopped
1 big Clove Garlic *(Lehsun)*–grated
1 teaspoon Minced Ginger and Green Chili *(Adrak-Hari Mirch)*
½ teaspoon Turmeric Powder *(Haldi)*
2 teaspoons Coriander Powder *(Dhaniya)*
½ teaspoon Red Chili Powder *(Lal Mirch)*
1½ teaspoons Salt *(Namak)*
½ teaspoon Roasted Cumin Powder *(Bhuna Zeera)*
½ teaspoon Mixed Spice *(Garam Masala)*
1 big Tomato *(Timatar)*–chopped
½ cup Tomato Juice *(Timatar Rus)*
2 cups Green Peas *(Hari Matar)*–fresh or frozen
3 cups Hot Tap Water (reduces cooking time)

Method:

Place the cottage cheese block on a board, then cut into 1 inch squares, and refrigerate overnight, so it is firmer. Heat 2 tablespoons oil in a non-stick pan, over low-medium heat, and shallow fry the cheese, for 2 minutes, until lightly golden.

Remove the cheese with a slotted spoon, and transfer on to a paper towel, leaving the excess oil in the pan. Transfer the oil from the pan into a medium pot, then add the remaining 2 tablespoons of oil to it.

Turn on the heat to medium, then add onions and sauté for 6-8 minutes, until golden brown. Add garlic and sauté for 30 seconds, until fragrant.

Reduce the heat to low-medium, and add the spices; ginger-green chili, turmeric, coriander, red chili, salt, cumin powder, and mixed spice, then sauté for a minute.

Add the tomato, and tomato juice, then mix well. Cover and cook, for about 10 minutes, over low-medium heat, until a thick sauce is formed, and the oil separates. Stir a few times. Allow the sauce to cool for 15 minutes, then transfer it to an electric blender and puree until smooth.

Transfer the sauce back in to the same pot, then add peas and ½ cup of water, and mix. Turn on the heat to medium-low; cover and cook, for 5 minutes, until they soften.

Add the remaining water and the cheese squares, then stir gently. Increase the heat to medium-high, and allow the curry to come to a boil. Reduce the heat back to medium. Cover and cook for about 10 minutes, until the cheese puffs up.

Then, reduce the heat to low-medium; partially cover and cook for another 30 minutes, or until the curry is thick, and oil separates.

Transfer the curry into a serving dish, and serve hot Matar Paneer with fresh kulcha, roti, parantha, or naan, accompanied with potato yogurt sauce, and onion relish.

Variations:

-To make *Cheese Dumplings*–*Paneer Kofta*; add 2 tablespoons all-purpose flour, ¼ teaspoon baking soda, and the spices to the cottage cheese, then knead to make smooth dough.

Divide the dough into 10 equal portions, and roll each into a round ball. Shallow fry those, until golden brown, then use in the curry.

-Substitute cheese with firm Tofu, to make a healthier dish.
-Add fresh or dry fenugreek leaves to the curry for additional flavor.

Mooli Baingan
(Radish Eggplant Curry)

Mooli Baingan is a north Indian *radish eggplant curry*, prepared from white radishes, and Japanese eggplants, cooked in an onion and tomato sauce. Radishes on their own, do not have much flavor, but when cooked with Indian spices, they taste sweeter and are delicious.

Serves 4
Ingredients:

Prep Time: 20 minutes
Cooking Time: 55 minutes

2 tablespoons Olive Oil *(Jaitoon Ka Tel)*
½ teaspoon Cumin Seeds *(Zeera)*
1 big Onion *(Pyaz)*–finely chopped
½ teaspoon Minced Ginger and Green Chili *(Adrak-Hari Mirch)*
1 teaspoon Turmeric Powder *(Haldi)*
2 teaspoons Salt *(Namak)*
½ teaspoon Red Chili Powder *(Lal Mirch)*
2 teaspoons Coriander Powder *(Dhaniya)*
½ teaspoon Roasted Cumin Powder *(Bhuna Zeera)*
2 Japanese Eggplants *(Baingan)*–cubed with skin, and soaked in water
1 long White Radish *(Mooli)*–peeled and cubed
¼ cup Hot Tap Water (reduces cooking time)
4 Roma Tomatoes *(Timatar)*–finely chopped
½ teaspoon Mixed Spice *(Garam Masala)*
2 tablespoons Chopped Cilantro *(Hara Dhaniya)*

Method:

Heat oil in a wok over medium heat, then add cumin seeds, and allow them to crackle. Add onions and sauté them for about 6-8 minutes, until golden brown.

Add ginger-green chili, turmeric, salt, red chili, coriander, and cumin powder, then cook for a minute. Strain the eggplants in a colander, and add to the spice mix along with the radish and water, then mix well.

Reduce the heat to low-medium, then cover and cook, for about 15 minutes, until the vegetables are soft. Add the tomatoes, then mix. Check the seasoning and add more as needed.

Cover and cook for about 15 more minutes, until the tomatoes are soft, and mushy, and the curry begins to thicken.

Partially cover and cook for another 10 minutes, until half of the moisture evaporates–the curry thickens, and the oil separates. Turn off the heat, and stir in the mixed spice. Cover, and allow the curry to sit for about 5 minutes so that the flavors infuse together.

Transfer the curry into a serving dish, and garnish with cilantro. Serve hot Mooli Baingan Curry with fresh roti, or parantha, accompanied with cucumber yogurt sauce, onion relish, and tomato chutney.

Variations:
-*Radish Greens Curry*–*Mooli Bhujia:* Substitute eggplant with white radish greens. Wash and chop the greens, then set them aside. Cook the radish, as in the recipe above, without the tomatoes. Stir-fry the greens in a separate pan, in little oil with a dash of salt and pepper, for about 2-3 minutes, until tender, but still have a bite to them, with a bright green color. Add the greens to the cooked radish, then mix, and serve.

-*Radish Potato Hash*–*Mooli Aloo Hash:* Substitute eggplant with 2 medium potatoes. Peel and grate the vegetables, then squeeze all their water content. Make a hash with 3 tablespoons oil, in a non-stick pan, over medium heat, for about 2 minutes on each side, until crispy golden. Squeeze some lemon juice, and a dash of salt and pepper on top. Cut in to wedges, then serve with mint and tamarind chutney.

Mooli Baingan *(Radish Eggplant Curry)*

Palak Paneer
(Spinach Cottage Cheese Curry)

Palak Paneer is a rich and creamy, *spinach cottage cheese curry*, prepared from fresh or frozen spinach, and homemade or store-bought cottage cheese. For this recipe, I have used fresh spinach, and fresh cottage cheese, which I prepared from 2% milk, to keep the dish lighter, without compromising the taste and flavor.

Serves 6
Ingredients:

Prep Time: 5 hours 5 minutes
Cooking Time: 1 hour 35 minutes

10 ounce block of Fresh Cottage Cheese *(Paneer)* Refer to Recipe on P111
4 tablespoons Olive Oil *(Jaitoon Ka Tel)*–divided
1 big Onion *(Pyaz)*–chopped
1 big Clove Garlic *(Lehsun)*–grated
1½ teaspoons Minced Ginger and Green Chili *(Adrak-Hari Mirch)*
1 teaspoon Turmeric Powder *(Haldi)*
1 teaspoon Salt *(Namak)*
½ teaspoon Red Chili Powder *(Lal Mirch)*
2 big Tomatoes *(Timatar)*–chopped
2 pounds Fresh Spinach *(Palak)*–washed, and chopped
2 cups Hot Tap Water (reduces cooking time)
1 teaspoon Mixed Spice *(Garam Masala)*

For Tempering:
2 tablespoons Olive Oil *(Jaitoon Ka Tel)*
2 tablespoons Unsalted Butter *(Makkhan)*
½ teaspoon Cumin Seeds *(Zeera)*

Method:
Place the block of cottage cheese on a cutting board, and cut into 1 inch squares, then refrigerate overnight, so it is firmer. Heat 2 tablespoons oil over low-medium heat in a non-stick pan, and shallow fry cheese in two batches, for 2-3 minutes each, until lightly golden on all sides. Remove cheese with a slotted spoon, on to a paper towel and set aside, leaving the excess oil in the pan.

Transfer the leftover oil from the pan into a big pot; then add the remaining 2 tablespoons of oil. Turn on the heat to medium, then add onions and sauté for about 6-8 minutes, until golden. Reduce the heat to low-medium, and add garlic, ginger-green chili, turmeric, salt, and red chili powder, then sauté for 1 minute.

Add tomatoes and cook, for 10 minutes, until they are soft and the oil separates. Add the spinach and the water, then mix. Increase the heat to medium-high, and allow the water to come to a boil.

Reduce the heat to low-medium. Cover and cook for about 20 minutes, until the spinach cooks and changes color to olive green, and the water reduces by half. Turn off the heat and set aside to cool for 15 minutes.

Puree the spinach mix in an electric blender, until smooth. Transfer it back into the same pot, then check the seasoning, and add more as needed. Turn on the heat to medium, then cover and cook the puree for 10 minutes, until it begins to bubble.

Reduce the heat to low-medium, then add cheese and gently mix. Partially cover and cook for 20 minutes, until the moisture reduces further, making the curry thicker–the cheese soft and spongy, and the oil separating. Stir in the mixed spice, then transfer the curry into a serving dish, and prepare the tempering.

For *tempering*, heat the oil and butter in a small pan over medium heat, then add the cumin seeds, and allow them to crackle. Give it a quick swirl and pour the tempering over the curry.

Serve hot Palak Paneer with naan, bhatura, or kulcha accompanied with roasted papadam, and onion relish.

Variations:
-Substitute cottage cheese with firm Tofu. Add 1 tablespoon fresh fenugreek leaves, and ¼ cup sour cream to the spinach curry for additional flavor and make a healthier dish.

-Substitute the spinach with baby swiss chard leaves, for similar flavor.

Palak Paneer *(Spinach Cottage Cheese Curry)*

Rasa Pakori
(Lentil Dumplings Curry)

Rasa Pakori is comfort food, and is prepared from split moong lentil dumplings, cooked in a spicy onion and tomato gravy.

Serves 6
Ingredients:

Prep Time: 13 hours 15 minutes
Cooking Time: 55 minutes

3 tablespoons Olive Oil *(Jaitoon Ka Tel)*
½ teaspoon Cumin Seeds *(Zeera)*
1 big Red Onion *(Pyaz)*–finely chopped
½ teaspoon Minced Ginger and Green Chili *(Adrak-Hari Mirch)*
½ teaspoon Turmeric Powder *(Haldi)*
2 teaspoons Coriander Powder *(Dhaniya)*
1 teaspoon Salt *(Namak)*
¼ teaspoon Red Chili Powder *(Lal Mirch)*
½ teaspoon Roasted Cumin Powder *(Bhuna Zeera)*
½ teaspoon Mixed Spice *(Garam Masala)*
2 big Tomatoes *(Timatar)*–finely chopped
½ cup Tomato Juice *(Timatar Rus)*
2 cups Hot Tap Water (reduces cooking time)
30 Small Moong Lentil Dumplings *(Moong Pakori)* Refer to Recipe on P52
1 tablespoon Chopped Cilantro *(Hara Dhaniya)*–for garnish

Method:.

Heat oil in a medium wide pot, over medium heat, then add cumin seeds and allow them to crackle. Add onions and sauté them for about 6-8 minutes, until golden.

Reduce the heat to low-medium, then add, ginger-green chili, turmeric, coriander, salt, red chili, cumin powder and mixed spice. Sauté for a minute, until aromatic.

Add tomatoes and tomato juice, then mix. Cover and cook, for 10 minutes, until tomatoes are soft and mushy, and the oil separates. Stir a few times in between to prevent burning.

Add water and mix well. Increase the heat to medium-high and allow the curry to come to a boil. Reduce the heat back to low-medium, and add the lentil dumplings, then gently stir. Cover and cook for 20 minutes, until they plump up, and the curry begins to thicken.

Reduce the heat further to low, then cover and cook for another 10 minutes, until the curry is thick enough to coat the dumplings.

Transfer the curry into a serving dish, and garnish with cilantro. Serve hot Rasa Pakori with roti or parantha, accompanied with onion relish, and roasted papadam.

Variations:
-Substitute the lentil dumplings with gram flour dumplings *(P91)*, then prepare the curry as in the recipe above. This cooks in less time.

Rasa Pakori *(Lentil Dumplings Curry) Recipe on P107*

Sarson Ka Saag *(Kale Spinach Collard Greens Curry)*

Sarson Ka Saag
(Kale Spinach Collard Greens Curry)

Sarson Ka Saag is a Punjabi dish, prepared from mustard leaves, spinach, and fenugreek leaves, and is eaten with Indian corn flatbread–*makki ki roti*. I make this dish, with kale–also called *mustard greens,* collard greens, and spinach leaves, which makes it creamier, more flavorful, and much lighter than the original recipe. This is a slow cooked, healthy, comfort food, but worth the wait, and warms your body in the winter.

Serves 8 *Prep Time: 25 minutes*
Ingredients: *Cooking Time: 2 hours 25 minutes*

3 tablespoons Olive Oil *(Jaitoon Ka Tel)*–divided
pinch of Asafoetida *(Heeing)*
1 teaspoon Cumin Seeds *(Zeera)*
1 teaspoon Minced Ginger and Green Chili *(Adrak-Hari Mirch)*
½ teaspoon Turmeric Powder *(Haldi)*
3 teaspoons Salt *(Namak)*
3 cups Hot Tap Water (reduces cooking time)
1 bunch fresh Kale *(Mustard Greens)*–washed and chopped
1 bunch fresh Collard Greens–washed and chopped
1 bunch fresh Spinach *(Palak)*–washed and chopped (or frozen spinach)
2 tablespoons Unsalted Butter *(Makkhan)*
4 heaped tablespoons Gram Flour *(Besan)*

For Tempering:
2 tablespoons Olive Oil *(Jaitoon Ka Tel)*
2 medium Onions *(Pyaz)*–finely chopped
2 big Cloves Garlic *(Lehsun)*–grated
½ teaspoon Turmeric Powder *(Haldi)*
1 teaspoon Red Chili Powder *(Lal Mirch)*
2 teaspoons Mango Powder *(Amchoor)*

For Garnish:
2 tablespoons Unsalted Butter *(Makkhan)*
1 Red Onion *(Lal Pyaz)*–sliced and pickled in lemon juice and salt
1 tablespoon Chopped Cilantro *(Hara Dhaniya)*

Method:
Heat 2 tablespoons of oil in a large, deep heavy base pot over medium heat. Add asafoetida, and allow it to sizzle. Add cumin seeds, and allow them to crackle. Reduce the heat to low-medium, and add ginger-green chili, turmeric, and salt, then sauté for a minute.

Add water and the prepared kale, collard greens, and spinach leaves, then mix. Increase heat to medium-high; and allow water to boil.

Reduce the heat to low-medium, then cover and cook for 45 minutes, until the greens are tender, and the water has reduced by half. Stir often. Turn off the heat and set the greens aside to cool for 15 minutes.

Transfer the greens mix to an electric blender, then pulse 3 times to make a coarse puree. Make the puree in 2-3 batches.

Melt the butter in the same pot over medium heat, and add the remaining oil to it, then add gram flour. Whisk and cook for 5 minutes, until the raw taste of flour minimizes, but does not turn brown. Add the puree back into the pot, and mix well, then cover and cook for 10 minutes, until it starts to bubble.

Reduce the heat to low, then cover and cook for 30 minutes, stirring often. Partially cover, and cook for another 30 minutes, until the moisture further reduces to one third; the curry becomes thicker and creamier. Stir often. Check the seasoning, and add more as needed.

For tempering, heat the oil in a shallow, pan over medium heat, then add onions and sauté for 6-8 minutes, until golden. Add garlic and sauté for another minute, until fragrant.

Add the dry spices–turmeric, red chili, and mango powder, then sauté for 30 seconds. Give a quick swirl and pour the tempering over the curry, then mix well.

Cover the curry for 10 minutes to allow all the flavors to infuse together, then transfer into a serving dish. Add the butter on top, for extra flavor and shine to the curry.

Garnish the curry with pickled red onions and cilantro, then serve hot Sarson Ka Saag with plain tava roti, accompanied with onion relish.

Variations:
-Add fresh fenugreek leaves to the greens mix for extra flavor.
-Add peeled and chopped white radish to the greens mix, while boiling, to bring additional flavor to the curry.
-Squeeze the juice of half a lemon with the garnish for some freshness.

How to Make Paneer
(How to Make Cottage Cheese)

Paneer in India is called *cottage cheese* around the world. It is a great source of protein for vegetarians, in the same way that meat is for non-vegetarians. Paneer is the easiest cheese that can be prepared at home, and fresh is the best. For this recipe, I have used whole milk to prepare the cheese. For low fat cheese, use 2% milk.

Makes 10 ounce (2 cups)
Ingredients:
½ gallon Whole Milk *(Doodh)*
6 tablespoons fresh Lemon Juice *(Neembu Rus)*
Also Needed:
A Heavy Base Pot
A Colander
Muslin or Cheese Cloth

Prep Time: 10 minutes
Cooking Time: 30 minutes
Inactive Time: 4 hours

Method:
Heat the milk in a heavy base pot, over medium-high heat, for about 10-12 minutes, until it comes to a boil. Stir constantly to prevent the milk from burning.

Reduce the heat to low, and stir in the lemon juice, 1 tablespoon at a time, until the milk curdles completely, and the cheese separates from the 'Whey'–*green water*. It takes about 8-10 minutes. Turn off the heat.

Strain the cheese, through a colander, lined with a fine muslin or cheese cloth, to drain the Whey. Then, wash the cheese with hands, under running water, for about 2 minutes, to eliminate the lemon flavor.

Bring together all four sides of the muslin cloth, then twist and squeeze out as much water as possible. Place the cheese, still wrapped in the muslin cloth, on a small sheet pan.

Place another sheet pan on top, and press down to flatten it. Further, to put more pressure, place a heavy weight on top of the sheet pan, such as a kettle full of water, then set aside for 4 hours, if the temperature is cool.

If the temperature is warm, refrigerate the pressed down cheese for 4 hours, and replace the kettle of water with a big yogurt container for the extra weight, until a flat round block of cheese has formed.

Remove the cheese from the muslin cloth and place it on a board. Cut it into 1 inch squares, then cover and refrigerate overnight, so it is firmer. Shallow fry the cheese in a little oil, for 2-3 minutes, until lightly golden on all sides. Refrigerate after cooling, for a few days, then freeze it for a longer period of time. Thaw, and use as needed.

Note: To make cheese from 2% milk, use 4 tablespoons of lemon juice.

Variations:
-Make *Cottage Cheese Flatbread*–*Paneer Ki Roti*, by kneading 1 cup cottage cheese, ½ teaspoon salt, and 1 tablespoon oil, in 1 cup wheat flour, with ¼ cup water, to make a soft, smooth pliable dough. Divide the dough into 6 equal portions. Then, follow the remaining steps as in the recipe for tava roti *(P166)*, to make the cheese flatbread.

-*Bake the Cheese* - Place it on a sheet pan, then coat the cheese with 2 tablespoons of olive oil, and bake at 400 degrees F, for 10 minutes, until lightly golden on all sides. Remove with a spatula, and use as needed.

-Use cheese in preparing curries, sandwiches, pizza, pasta, fritters, or just eat plain, when freshly made with a dash of salt.

-Use 'Whey' from the cheese, in preparing healthier soups, and stews.

Paneer *(Homemade Cottage Cheese)*

Aloo Tikki
(Potato Cutlet)

Aloo Tikki is *potato cutlet*–one of the most delicious snacks I know. It is prepared from boiled potato cutlets, stuffed with or without lentil-peas filling. For this recipe, I have prepared plain, deep fried potato cutlets.

Serves 6, Makes 12 *Prep Time: 40 minutes*
Ingredients: *Cooking Time: 35 minutes*

6 medium Potatoes *(Aloo)*
2-3 cups Hot Tap Water (reduces boiling time)
1 tablespoon Arrowroot Powder *(Ararot)* or Corn Starch
2 Slices White or Wheat Bread–moistened and squeezed
1 teaspoon Minced Ginger and Green Chili *(Adrak-Hari Mirch)*
1 teaspoon Salt *(Namak)*
½ teaspoon Red Chili Powder *(Lal Mirch)*
1 cup Vegetable Oil–for frying
2 tablespoons Chopped Cilantro *(Hara Dhaniya)*
Stuffing: (optional)
¼ cup Split Moong Lentils *(Moong Dhuli)*, plus 1 cup Hot Water
½ cup Green Peas *(Hari Matar)*–fresh or frozen
¼ teaspoon Salt *(Namak)*
¼ teaspoon Red Chili Powder *(Lal Mirch)*
1 tablespoon Vegetable Oil

Method:
Wash and prick the potatoes, then microwave them in 2 cups water, for 10-12 minutes; or boil in 3 cups water on the stove top, for 20-25 minutes, until soft. Strain the potatoes, and allow cooling for 15 minutes, then peel, and mash them.

Add the arrowroot or corn starch to the potatoes, then lightly knead to make smooth dough *(Kneading too hard will make it stringy, and sticky)*. Set aside to cool. *(Arrowroot prevents the cutlets from breaking while frying)*.

For Stuffing: Soak the lentils in water, for 1 hour, then strain. Coarsely grind them in a food processor with a little water. Heat the oil in a non-stick pan over low-medium heat, then stir-fry the lentils, for 5 minutes.

Add the peas and stir-fry for 5 minutes, until tender. Add salt and red chili powder, then stir-fry for a few more minutes, until it smells roasted. Mash the peas with a fork, to make a coarse mix.

Break the moist bread slices into very small pieces, then add to the potato dough. Add ginger-green chili, salt, red chili, and half the cilantro, then gently mix, until well combined. Check the seasoning, and add more as needed. Divide the dough, into 12 equal portions, then roll each into a round ball. Set them aside on a plate, lined with parchment paper.

With Stuffing: Take each potato ball, and make a dip in the center, to spoon in ½ teaspoon of the stuffing mix. Close and seal, then gently roll again and lightly press, to flatten it. Stuff the remaining balls, and place them back on the plate, then cover loosely with a damp paper towel.

Without Stuffing: Roll and press the potato balls without the stuffing, then follow the steps below to shallow fry or deep fry them.

To Shallow Fry: Heat 4 tablespoons of oil, in a non-stick pan, over medium heat. Place 4 potato cutlets in the oil, then lightly press and fry for 2 minutes on each side, until golden and crispy on both sides. Add a little more oil, as needed. Remove the cutlets with a spatula, and transfer on to a paper towel to drain excess oil. Repeat, until all cutlets are fried.

To Deep Fry: Heat 1 cup oil in a wok, over medium heat. Carefully slide 4 cutlets in the oil, and fry for 2 minutes on each side, until golden on all sides. Remove with a slotted spoon and transfer on to a paper towel, to drain excess oil.

Repeat, until all cutlets are fried. Transfer the cutlets on to a serving platter, then garnish with remaining cilantro. Serve hot Aloo Tikki with tamarind and mint chutney, or tomato ketchup.

Variations:
-*To bake:* Brush the cutlets with a little oil, then bake at 350 degrees F, for 12 minutes, until golden on all sides. This is a healthier version.
-Use cutlets in making potato burgers with lettuce, tomatoes, red onion rings, mint chutney and tomato ketchup.

Subzi Pakoras
(Vegetable Fritters)

Subzi Pakoras are *vegetable fritters* prepared from marinated vegetables, coated in gram flour batter, and then deep fried. These are full of flavor, and can be eaten for breakfast or with evening tea, and also in a sandwich for a light lunch or dinner.

Serves 4
Ingredients:

Prep time: 30 minutes
Cooking Time: 25 minutes

For Rub:
1 teaspoon Salt *(Namak)*–divided
½ teaspoon Red Chili Powder *(Lal Mirch)*–divided
½ teaspoon Ground Black Pepper *(Kali Mirch)*–divided
½ teaspoon Carom Seeds *(Ajwain)*–divided

Vegetables for Fritters:
1 medium Eggplant, 1 Potato, 1 Red Onion *(Baingan, Aloo, Lal Pyaz)*

For Batter:
1½ cups Gram Flour *(Besan)*
1 tablespoon Corn Starch
½ teaspoon Minced Ginger and Green Chili *(Adrak-Hari Mirch)*
1 tablespoon Chopped Cilantro *(Hara Dhaniya)*
1 tablespoon Chopped Chives *(Hara Pyaz)*
¼ cup Water–for batter–add more as needed

Also Needed: 1½ cups Vegetable Oil–for frying

Method:
In a medium bowl, combine and mix, half each salt, red chili, black pepper, and carom seeds *(crush the carom seeds between your palms to release their oil)*. Slice the eggplant and potato with the skin, into thin rounds. Peel and cut the onion into thick slices, keeping the rings together.

Sprinkle the rub mix on the vegetables, then gently and nicely massage them, until well coated. Cover and set aside for 10 minutes to marinate. Marinating vegetables brings lots of flavor to the fritters.

In another medium bowl, combine chick pea flour, corn starch, ginger-green chili, cilantro, chives, and remaining salt, red chili, black pepper, and carom seeds. Check the seasoning, and add more as needed.

Slowly add water while whisking, to form smooth thick batter, which coats the back of a spoon. Cover and set aside for 10 minutes.

Heat the oil, in a wok or a karahi, over medium heat. Test the oil by dropping a little batter in it, which should sizzle and rise to the top in 30 seconds, and not turn brown.

Add 4 marinated vegetable slices at a time, to the batter, coating them well. Use kitchen tongs to shake off the extra batter, then carefully slide each slice into the hot oil. Fry them for 2 minutes on each side, until lightly golden and crispy.

Remove the fritters with a slotted spoon, on to a paper towel to drain excess oil. Repeat, until all the fritters are fried.

Transfer the fritters on to a serving platter. Then, serve hot Subzi Pakoras with mint and tamarind chutney. Delicious!

Variations:
-For *Chicken or Fish Fritters*–*Murg or Machchi Pakora,* substitute the vegetables with boneless chicken or fish pieces. Use all-purpose flour instead of gram flour for the batter, because it is lighter and goes well with chicken and fish. Season with salt and pepper to taste.

Top: Aloo Pakoras
(Potato Fritters)
Center: Baingan Pakoras
(Eggplant Fritters)
Bottom: Pyaz Pakoras
(Onion Fritters)

Kurkuree Hari Phali
(Crispy Green Beans)

Kurkuree Hari Phali are *crispy green beans*–a delicious and healthy snack. These crispy beans are light, flavorful, and very easy to make. They are always eaten fresh, so fry them just before it is time to eat.

Serves 6
Ingredients:

Prep Time: 20 minutes
Cooking Time: 20 minutes

1 cup All-Purpose Flour *(Maida)*
1 cup Low-Fat Buttermilk *(Chaach)*
1 tablespoon Corn Starch
¼ teaspoon Minced Ginger and Green Chili *(Adrak-Hari Mirch)*
½ teaspoon Salt *(Namak)*
½ teaspoon Red Chili Powder *(Lal Mirch)*
¼ teaspoon Garlic Powder
¼ teaspoon Onion Powder
2 tablespoons Bread Crumbs
1 tablespoon Chopped, Cilantro *(Hara Dhaniya)*
2 tablespoons Water
1 cup Vegetable Oil–for frying
1 pound Fresh Green Beans *(Hari Phali)*–washed, trimmed, pat dried

Method:

In a medium bowl, combine flour, butter milk, corn starch, ginger-green chili, salt, red chili, garlic and onion powder, bread crumbs, half the cilantro, and water.

Whisk to form smooth batter, then cover and set aside, for 10 minutes. If the batter is too thick, add a few more teaspoons of water, then mix.

Heat the oil in a wok, or a karahi, over medium heat. Then, test the oil by dropping a little batter in it, which should sizzle, and rise to the top, in 30 seconds, and not turn brown.

Dip 5 green beans in the batter at a time, and coat them well. Then, with kitchen tongs, shake off the extra batter, and drop them in the oil separately, without letting them touch each other while frying.

Fry for 2 minutes, until lightly golden on all sides. Remove with a slotted spoon on to a paper towel, to drain excess oil.

Repeat the process, until all green beans are fried. Transfer them on to a serving platter, then garnish with remaining cilantro and a sprinkle of salt and pepper. Serve hot Kurkuree Hari Phali with tamarind and mint chutney or tomato ketchup.

Note: Fry them just before serving time so they stay fresh and crispy.

Kurkuree Hari Phali *(Crispy Green Beans) Recipe on P117*

Sooji Dhokla *(Savory Semolina Cake)*

Sooji Dhokla
(Savory Semolina Cake)

Dhokla is a spongy and *savory semolina cake*. It is a Gujarati dish, originally prepared from a fermented batter of rice and chick peas, which takes longer to prepare. I use coarse semolina, to make an instant version, which is lighter, flavorful, and gets ready in much less time.

Serves 8
Ingredients:
For Batter: Makes 2 Cakes

Prep Time: 10 minutes
Cooking Time: 50 minutes
Inactive Time: 25 minutes

1 cup Coarse Semolina *(Sooji)*
1 cup Plain Non-Fat Greek Yogurt *(Dahi)*
1 teaspoon Lemon Juice *(Neembu Rus)*
¼ teaspoon Turmeric Powder *(Haldi)*
1 teaspoon Salt *(Namak)*
1 teaspoon Minced Ginger and Green Chili *(Adrak-Hari Mirch)*
2 teaspoons Vegetable Oil
¼ cup Water
1 teaspoon ENO Fruit Salt (from Indian Store) or Baking Soda–divided

Also Needed:
1 Deep Pot, plus 2 cups Water–for steaming
1 Cake Rack *(or Cake Pan, placed upside down)*
2 round non-stick Cake Pans– size 8 by 8 by 2 inch
2 teaspoons Vegetable Oil–for greasing the pans–divided

For Tempering:
2 teaspoons Vegetable Oil
½ teaspoon Mustard Seeds *(Rai)*
¼ teaspoon Red Chili Powder *(Lal Mirch)*

For Garnish: 1 tablespoon Chopped Cilantro *(Hara Dhaniya)*

Method:
In a medium bowl, combine semolina, yogurt, lemon juice, turmeric, salt, ginger-green chili, oil, and water, then whisk to form a smooth batter. Cover and set aside to rest for 15 minutes. Meanwhile, boil 2 cups of water in the deep pot, over low-medium heat, with the cake rack already placed inside it, on the bottom, and in the center.

Add ½ teaspoon of ENO salt, or baking soda, to half the batter, and mix quickly. Then, transfer it into the first, pregreased cake pan, up to half the depth of the pan, leaving enough room for it to rise.

Tap the pan to level the batter, and place it on top of the cake rack inside the pot, then close it with the lid. *The ENO salt (or baking soda) helps the batter rise.* Steam for 15 minutes over medium-high heat, then turn off the heat. Wait for a few minutes, then open the lid.

Lightly press the semolina cake, and it should spring back. Remove the cake pan and set aside to cool for 10 minutes.

Meanwhile, add the remaining ½ teaspoon of ENO salt to the rest of the batter, then prepare the second batch of semolina cake.

For *tempering*, heat the oil in a small pan over medium heat, then add mustard seeds, and allow them to crackle. Add red chili powder, and give a quick swirl, then pour over the semolina cakes in circular motion. It makes a sizzling sound.

Garnish the cakes with cilantro, then cut into 2 inch squares. Transfer them on to a serving platter and serve Sooji Dhokla with mint and tamarind chutney, accompanied with a cup of tea.

Tip: You can also use a pressure cooker without the weight on top, and replacing it with a small bowl to block the hole, then steam the dhokla for 15 minutes. *This allows the steam to escape slowly and prevents any pressure building up inside the cooker; and that is the right way.*

Sooji Dhokla Squares *(Savory Semolina Cake Squares)*

Sooji Upma
(Semolina Polenta)

Sooji Upma is a common South Indian breakfast dish, similar to polenta. It is prepared from roasted semolina–also called *Rava* in India; vegetables, and spices. My mother used to prepare this dish with evening tea, and it tasted delicious. For this recipe, I have used green peas with semolina.

Serves 2 *Prep Time: 10 minutes*
Ingredients: *Cooking Time: 25 minutes*

½ cup Coarse Semolina *(Sooji /Rava)*
3 tablespoons Olive Oil *(Jaitoon Ka Tel)*–divided
1½ cups Water
½ teaspoon Mustard Seeds *(Rai)*
½ medium Onion *(Pyaz)*–finely chopped
1 teaspoon Salt *(Namak)*
¼ teaspoon Red Chili Powder *(Lal Mirch)*
1 teaspoon Minced Ginger and Green Chili *(Adrak-Hari Mirch)*
½ cup Frozen Green Peas *(Hari Matar)*–thawed
1 tablespoon Unsalted Butter *(Makkhan)*

Method:

In a medium saucepan, roast the semolina in 1 tablespoon of oil, over low-medium heat. Constantly stir the semolina, for about 5 minutes, until lightly golden, with a strong roasted aroma.

Remove from heat, and transfer into a bowl. Allow it to cool for 5 minutes, then add water, and whisk to a smooth blend, with no lumps.

In the same pan, heat the remaining 2 tablespoons of oil, over medium heat. Add mustard seeds, and allow them to crackle.

Add onions and sauté for about 6-8 minutes, until golden. Reduce the heat to low-medium, and add salt, red chili powder, and ginger-green chili, then sauté for 30 seconds.

Add peas, and 2 tablespoons of water, from the semolina blend, then mix well. Cover and cook for 2 minutes, until peas are tender, but still crunchy, with a bright green color.

Whisk the semolina blend once, then add it to the peas and onion mix, while stirring, to prevent forming lumps. Continue to stir, holding the lid on top, over low heat, for about 6-8 minutes, until it bubbles and thickens; the oil separates, and polenta leaves the edges of the pot. *The lid prevents the polenta from splashing everywhere.*

Turn off the heat, and transfer Sooji Upma into a serving dish. Add butter on top to make it creamier and more flavorful.

Eat for breakfast, brunch or as an evening snack. It is delicious!!

Variations:
-Add boiled potatoes to the polenta to make it hearty.
-Add soaked and boiled gram lentils before adding the semolina blend. Sauté for 2 minutes, then add semolina mix and cook as in the recipe.

Meetha Dalia *(Sweet Cream of Wheat)*

Meetha Dalia
(Sweet Cream of Wheat)

Meetha Dalia is roasted *sweet cream of wheat,* prepared from cracked wheat, cooked in sugar syrup with nuts and flavorings. It is eaten for breakfast in India; is very good for health, and full of protein and fiber.

Serves 4 *Prep Time: 10 minutes*
Ingredients: *Cooking Time: 40 minutes*

2 tablespoons Canola/Vegetable Oil
1 cup Coarse Cream of Wheat *(Dalia)*
4 cups Hot Tap Water (reduces cooking time)
6 tablespoons Sugar *(Chini)*
½ teaspoon Cardamom Powder *(Ilaichi)*
1/3 cup Slivered Almonds, Cashews, Raisins *(Badam, Kaju, Kishmish)*
1 teaspoon Slivered Almonds *(Badam)*–for garnish

Method:
Heat the oil in a medium saucepan, over medium heat, then roast the cream of wheat, for about 5-7 minutes, stirring constantly, until it looks like white dots and smells roasted. Remove from heat.

Wear oven mitts, and slowly add water to the hot wheat. It will bubble and form steam. Bring it back to heat and mix well. Remove mitts.

Increase the heat to medium-high and allow water to boil. Reduce the heat to low-medium, then cover and cook for 15-20 minutes, until wheat is tender, but not mushy. Stir a few times to prevent burning.

Add sugar, mixed nuts, and cardamom, then mix again. Partially cover and cook for 10 more minutes, until sugar dissolves–most of the water evaporates, and raisins plump up.

Transfer Sweet Cream of Wheat into a serving bowl. Garnish with slivered almonds, and serve hot. *Add a little water when reheating the leftovers.*

Variations:
-*Savory Cream of Wheat*: Substitute sugar with salt to taste, then cook as in recipe above. For tempering, heat a little oil with ¼ teaspoon cumin seeds crackling, and ¼ teaspoon red chili. Pour over Dalia.
-*Cook with Milk and Sugar*: Substitute water with milk; then follow the remaining cooking steps as in the recipe for meetha dalia above.

Bandgobhi Bonda
(Cabbage Dumplings)

Bandgobhi Bonda or *cabbage dumplings,* are a light and flavorful vegetable snack, cooked without the batter. These are prepared from shredded cabbage, boiled potatoes, and spices, then deep fried.

Serves 2-3 *Prep Time: 20 minutes*
Ingredients: *Cooking Time: 7 minutes*
For Dumplings: Makes 8
2 cups Shredded Cabbage *(Bandgobhi)*–squeezed to remove water content
2 medium Potatoes *(Aloo)*–boiled, peeled and mashed
½ cup Minced Onion *(Pyaz)*
½ inch Green Chili *(Hari Mirch)*–minced
½ inch Fresh Ginger *(Adrak)*–minced
½ cup Bread Crumbs
3 Slices of Wheat Bread–moistened, squeezed and shredded
1½ teaspoons Salt *(Namak)*
½ teaspoon Red Chili Powder *(Lal Mirch)*
1 tablespoon Chopped Cilantro *(Hara Dhaniya)*
1 tablespoon Olive Oil *(Jaitoon Ka Tel)*

Also Needed:
3 tablespoons dry All-Purpose Flour *(Maida)*–for rolling
1 cup Vegetable Oil–for frying
A sprig of Cilantro *(Hara Dhaniya)*–for garnish

Method:
In a medium bowl, combine cabbage, potatoes, onions, green chili, ginger, bread crumbs, bread slices, salt, red chili, cilantro, and oil, then scrunch and mix to form smooth soft dough. Divide the dough into 8 equal portions. Roll each into a round ball.

Dip each ball into the dry flour, and coat with it. Lightly roll them all again, shaking off extra flour, then set aside to rest for 5 minutes.

Meanwhile, heat the oil in a wok over medium heat. Check the oil by dropping a small piece of dough in it, which should sizzle and rise to the top in 30 seconds, and not turn brown.

Place 4 dumplings in a slotted spoon, and carefully slide them into the hot oil. Don't touch them, until lightly golden on the underside.

Gently turn them over, and allow them to turn golden on the other side too, for about 3 minutes in total.

Remove with a slotted spoon on to a paper towel to drain the excess oil. Repeat, until all dumplings are fried.

Transfer them on to a serving platter, and garnish with cilantro. Serve hot Bandgobhi Bonda with mint and tamarind chutney.

These bandgobhi bondas are crispy on the outside, soft on the inside, and have a kick to them. Enjoy!!

Variations:
-Add green peas, grated cauliflower, spinach or any other vegetable to the bonda mix for additional flavors.

-*Potato Dumplings*–*Aloo Bonda:* Use boiled and mashed potatoes for the dumplings; coat them with seasoned gram flour batter, then deep fry.

-*Cabbage Dumplings with Batter*: Prepare the dumplings as in the recipe above, without frying. Then, coat them with seasond all-purpose flour, or gram flour batter, and deep fry, until golden on all sides.

-*For Batter:* Combine ½ cup gram flour or all-purpose flour, ¼ teaspoon each salt, red chili and ginger powder, carom seeds, black pepper and 1 teaspoon corn starch, in a medium bowl. Add a little water and whip to make a smooth, thick batter. Use it to coat the dumplings and fry.

Bandgobhi Bonda *(Cabbage Dumplings)*

Neembu Cheeley
(Lemon Crepes)

Neembu Cheeley are *lemon crepes*–light, soft, and delicious with lemon flavor. This recipe has no eggs and it tastes delicious.

Serves 4, Makes 10
Ingredients:
Prep Time: 10 minutes
Cooking Time: 30 minutes

1 cup All-Purpose Flour *(Maida)*
½ cup Sour Cream
¼ teaspoon Salt *(Namak)*
1 teaspoon Baking Soda
2 tablespoons Vegetable Oil
1 cup Water
½ cup Vegetable Oil–for cooking
1 Lemon *(Neembu)*–cut into quarters
¾ cup Sugar *(Chini)*–to sprinkle

Method:
Combine flour, sour cream, salt, baking soda, and 2 tablespoons oil, in a medium bowl, then mix well. Slowly whisk in the water, to make a smooth batter. Cover and set aside for 5 minutes to rest.

Brush 1 tablespoon oil evenly on the base of a non-stick pan, then turn on the heat to medium. Wait for 1 minute, then pour ¼ cup batter into the pan. Tilt the pan, so the batter coats the base evenly.

Cook for 1 minute, or until it is lightly golden on the underside. Then, lift the edges with a spatula, and flip the crepe. Cook for 1 minute on the other side, then flip back, and transfer on to a plate.

Squeeze some lemon juice all over the crepe, and sprinkle some sugar, then fold into half, and again into half, to make a triangle. Garnish with a little more sugar and the remaining lemon quarters, then serve hot. Repeat, to make more crepes, until the batter is finished.

Variations:
-Stuff fresh strawberries or blueberries with sugar, in the center of the crepe, and roll it like a log; then top it with whipped cream.
-Make a strawberry or blueberry chunky sauce, and pour over crepes; then top it with a dollop of whipped cream. I love it!

Neembu Cheeley *(Lemon Crepes)*

Battered Bonda *(Battered Dumplings) Recipe on P125*

Vegetable Samosa
(Vegetable Stuffed Pastry)

Vegetable Samosa is a popular Indian snack prepared from an all-purpose flour pastry, stuffed with spicy potato and peas mix. This is an easy to make snack, and can be prepared in advance, and stored in an airtight container in the freezer, or refrigerated a day before using it.

Serves 6, Makes 12
Ingredients:
For Pastry:

Prep Time: 20 minutes
Cooking Time: 50 minutes
Inactive Time: 20 minutes

1 cup All-Purpose Flour *(Maida)*
2 tablespoons, plus 1 teaspoon Vegetable Oil
¼ teaspoon Salt *(Namak)*
½ cup Water
½ cup Flour *(Maida)*–for rolling
1 cup Vegetable Oil–for frying

For Filling:
3 tablespoons Vegetable Oil
1 teaspoon Minced Ginger and Green Chili *(Adrak-Hari Mirch)*
1 teaspoon Coriander Powder *(Dhaniya)*
½ teaspoon Red Chili Powder *(Lal Mirch)*
½ teaspoon Salt *(Namak)*
1 teaspoon Roasted Cumin Powder *(Bhuna Zeera)*
½ teaspoon Mixed Spice *(Garam Masala)*
1/3 cup Green Peas *(Hari Matar)*–frozen (thawed) or fresh
2 large Potatoes *(Aloo)*–boiled, peeled, small cubed
1 teaspoon Mango Powder *(Amchoor)*
1 tablespoon Chopped Cilantro *(Hara Dhaniya)*

Also Needed:
Cast Iron Griddle *(Tava)*
2 tablespoons flour, plus ¼ cup Water–for making the sealing paste

Method:
For Pastry: Combine 1 cup flour 2 tablespoons oil and salt, in a medium bowl, then mix well. Add water a little at a time, and knead for 5-8 minutes, until a smooth pliable dough has formed.

Apply 1 teaspoon oil to the dough, and knead again for a few minutes. Then, cover and set aside for 20 minutes, or refrigerate if it is too warm.

For Filling: Heat oil in a medium saucepan over low-medium heat. Add ginger-green chili, coriander, red chili, salt, cumin, and mixed spice, then stir-fry for a minute.

Add peas and stir-fry for 2 minutes, or until they are soft. Add potatoes, mango powder, and cilantro, then mix, and cook for 2 more minutes. Check the seasoning, and add more as needed, then set aside to cool.

To Make Samosa: Divide the dough into 6 equal portions, then roll and press each portion between your palms, into a round–flat disc. Set aside on a plate, and cover them with a moist paper towel to prevent drying.

Turn on the griddle to low heat. Then, dust the kitchen counter with some dry flour, and using a rolling pin, roll one disc into a 6 inch round. Flip it between your hands, and place it on the warm griddle.

Cook the round for 30 seconds on each side, then remove and place it on a plate lined with a moist paper towel. Cover it with another moist paper towel, to prevent drying. Repeat, until all rounds are lightly cooked. Then, turn off the heat.

Take one round and cut it in the center into 2 equal halves. Use one half, and put back the other one under the moist paper towel.

Apply a little sealing paste along the diameter of the half-round. Hold the half-round with both hands, and turn it around with your fingers to make a cone; then overlap and seal the edges securely.

Spoon a tablespoon of filling into the opening of the cone, and close the 2 bottom edges by applying more sealing paste, then overlapping and sealing them securely. Repeat, to fill remaining samosas; then set aside.

Heat oil in a wok, over medium heat. Test the oil by dropping a small piece of dough in it, which should sizzle and rise to the top in 30 seconds, and not turn brown. Carefully slide 4 samosas at a time into the oil, and fry for 2 minutes on each side, until lightly golden all over.

Reduce the heat to low, and remove them with a slotted spoon, on to a plate lined with a paper towel, to drain excess oil. Repeat, to fry the remaining samosas. Transfer on to a serving platter, then serve hot Vegetable Samosa with mint and tamarind chutney or tomato ketchup.

Variations:
-Substitute vegetable filling with keema masala *(P152)*, for making the *Keema Masala Stuffed Pastry*–*Keema Samosa.*

-*Vegetable Stuffed Tortilla*–*Tortilla Samosa:* Substitute regular pastry with tortilla pastry, then follow the remaining steps for stuffing and frying the samosa as stated above.

-*For Filling*: -Add sautéed onions to the potatoes and peas mix.
 -Make with sautéed onions and potatoes, without peas.
-Make with sautéed onions, potatoes, and spinach.
-Make with onions, garlic, green beans, carrots, and potatoes.

-*Pastry Crisps*–*Matthi:* Roll the leftover dough into a big round shape; then cut into 2 inch long stripes. Fry them in the same oil over medium heat, for 2-3 minutes, or until lightly golden on all sides. Drain them on to a plate lined with a paper towel, and eat warm, or at room temperature; with or without chutney. They are good as a light evening snack.

-*Baked Spinach Stuffed Filo Pastry*–*Palak Filo Samosa:* Add 1 teaspoon vinegar, 1 tablespoon olive oil, and 1 teaspoon lemon juice, to 1 cup flour, then knead with 1/8 cup warm water, for 15-20 minutes, to form a pliable dough. Cover with a plastic wrap and refrigerate overnight before using. Roll and fill the pastry as in vegetable samosa recipe. Bake at 350 degrees F, for 12 minutes, or until lightly golden.

Vegetable Samosa *(Vegetable Stuffed Pastry)*

Matthi *(Pastry Crisps)*

Tortilla Samosa *(Vegetables Stuffed Tortilla)*

Baked Namak Paare
(Baked Savory Squares)

Baked Namak Paare are *baked savory squares*, prepared from white and wheat flour dough, then baked; keeping them lighter, and healthier with better flavor. Original recipe asks for deep frying them.

Makes 6 cups
Ingredients:
1 cup All-Purpose Flour *(Maida)*
1 cup Wheat Flour *(Roti Atta)*
¼ cup, plus 2 teaspoons Vegetable Oil
1 teaspoon Salt *(Namak)*
½ teaspoon Carom Seeds *(Ajwain)*–crush between palms to release oil
½ teaspoon Freshly Ground Black Pepper *(Pisi Kali Mirch)*
1 teaspoon Baking Powder
½ cup Water

Prep Time: 15 minutes
Cooking Time: 1 hour 40 minutes
Inactive Time: 15 minutes

Method:
Combine white and wheat flour, oil, salt, carom seeds, black pepper, and baking powder in a medium bowl, then mix. Add water a little at a time, and knead to make smooth pliable dough. Cover with a damp paper towel and set aside for 10 minutes.

Turn on the oven at 350 degrees F. Dust the surface with white or wheat flour, then divide the dough into 3 equal portions. Work with one portion, while keeping the other two covered with the damp paper towel to prevent drying.

Use a rolling pin to roll the dough into a 10 by 10 inch square shape with 1/8 inch thickness, then cut it into 1 inch small squares.

Place them on to a sheet pan, lined with parchment paper. Re-roll the uneven ends of the dough to make more squares. Place the sheet pan on the middle rack in the oven, then bake for 7 minutes. Turn around the sheet pan, and bake for 7 more minutes, until lightly golden on all sides.

Remove and allow them to rest for 5 minutes, then transfer on to another sheet pan to completely cool. They get one shade darker after cooling, so remove them when they are a light golden color.

Repeat the process with the remaining two portions of the dough, until they are finished, and baked. When completely cool, store them in a cookie jar or a plastic container. Serve at room temperature.

Variations:

Sweet Squares–*Shakkar Paare:* Substitute the salt, pepper, and carom seeds with ¾ cup sugar, and 3 teaspoons of fennel seeds. Other ingredients stay as same. Follow the steps to prepare the dough; then roll and bake the sweet squares as in the recipe above.

Baked Namak Paare *(Baked Savory Squares)*

Grilled Hash Sandwich *(Recipe on P137)*

Subzi Roll
(Vegetable Roll)

Subzi Roll is a delicious vegetable snack item, prepared from stuffing a bread slice with a spicy mix of peas and potato filling; then shallow fried.

Serves 6, Makes 6
Ingredients:

Prep Time: 15 minutes
Cooking Time: 50 minutes

2 tablespoons Olive Oil *(Jaitoon Ka Tel)*
1 medium Onion *(Pyaz)*–finely chopped
1 teaspoon Minced Ginger and Green Chili *(Adrak-Hari Mirch)*
½ teaspoon Salt *(Namak)*
½ teaspoon Red Chili Powder *(Lal Mirch)*
½ teaspoon Roasted Cumin Powder *(Bhuna Zeera)*
½ teaspoon Mango Powder *(Amchoor)*
¼ teaspoon Mixed Spice *(Garam Masala)*
½ cup Frozen Green Peas *(Hari Matar)*–thawed
2 medium Potatoes *(Aloo)*–boiled, peeled and mashed
1 tablespoon Chopped Cilantro *(Hara Dhaniya)*
6 Slices Wheat or White Bread–one day old firm bread
1 cup Water
½ cup Canola Oil–for shallow frying

Method:
Heat the oil in a medium skillet over medium heat. Add onions and sauté, for 6-8 minutes, until golden. Then, add ginger-green chili and sauté for 1 minute, until fragrant.

Reduce the heat to low, and add salt, red chili, cumin powder, mango powder, and mixed spice, then sauté for a minute. Add peas and give a quick stir. Cover and cook for 2 minutes, until tender.

Add the potatoes, and cilantro; then fold them into the pea's mix, until everything incorporates well.

Check the seasoning, and add more as needed *(keep the mix extra spicy, as it tastes milder after stuffed in the bread)*. Then, set aside for 10 minutes.

To prepare the rolls, trim the edges of the bread slices, then cover and set them aside. Take one slice and moisten it by lightly dipping one side in water. Then, squeeze it between your palms to remove excess water.

Place 1 tablespoon of filling, diagonally, in the center of the slice, then gently lift and hold it with both hands. Fold all the sides of the slice towards the center, overlapping each other, wrapping the filling inside.

Gently press and squeeze the vegetable roll, to remove the remaining water content, closing the edges securely, making it into an oval shape. Repeat, to make the remaining rolls, until all are done. Set them aside for 5 minutes to rest.

Heat the oil in a skillet, over medium heat. Shallow fry 2 rolls at a time, for 2-3 minutes, until lightly golden all around. Remove them with a slotted spoon onto a paper towel to drain excess oil.

Repeat and fry the remaining rolls until all are done. Transfer the rolls onto a serving platter, and serve hot Subzi Rolls as an evening snack with mint and tamarind chutney or tomato ketchup.

Variations:
-*Cocktail Vegetable Roll*: Cut each trimmed bread slice, into half, making two small rectangles. Moisten and squeeze one half, then place the filling vertically in the center. Follow the remaining steps as in the recipe above, to make the cocktail rolls.
-*Filling*: Sauté the bean sprouts, and julienned carrots, red bell peppers, green beans, and scallions in oil and spices, then use as filling for rolls.

Subzi Roll *(Vegetable Roll)*

Shakarkandi Makai Hash
(Sweet Potato Corn Hash)

Shakarkandi Makai Hash is a mix of spicy, stir-fried vegetables, called *sweet potato corn hash*. It is a flavorful dish, and can be eaten either as a snack or as a light meal by stuffing in a grilled sandwich.

Serves 4   *Prep Time: 45 Minutes*
Ingredients: *Cooking Time: 35 minutes*

5 tablespoons Olive Oil *(Jaitoon Ka Tel)*–divided
1 large Red Onion *(Lal Pyaz)*–chopped
1 big Clove Garlic *(Lehsun)*–grated
1 inch Green Chili *(Hari Mirch)*–minced
1 inch Ginger *(Adrak)*–minced
1 cup Fresh Corn Kernels *(Makai)*
1 large Sweet Potato *(Shakarkandi)*–washed and cubed with skin
2 teaspoons Salt *(Namak)*
1 Green Bell Pepper *(Hari Shimla Mirch)*–deseeded and cubed
1 Red Bell Pepper *(Lal Shimla Mirch)*–deseeded and cubed
½ teaspoon Red Chili Powder *(Lal Mirch)*
½ teaspoon Roasted Cumin Powder *(Bhuna Zeera)*
1 teaspoon Crushed Black Pepper *(Kuti Kali Mirch)*
½ teaspoon Crushed Red Pepper Flakes *(Kuti Lal Mirch)*–divided
2 medium Potatoes *(Aloo)*–half boiled, peeled and cubed
½ Lemon *(Neembu)*
Also Needed: A Wok

Method:
Heat 3 tablespoons oil in the wok over medium heat. Add onions, and stir-fry for 5 minutes, until lightly golden.

Reduce the heat to low-medium, and add garlic, green chili, ginger, and corn kernels. Keep stir-frying, for 5 minutes, until corn is tender, but still has a crunch to it.

Add sweet potato cubes and salt, then stir-fry, for 5 minutes, until they are tender, but still hold their shape. Add green and red bell peppers and stir-fry for 3 minutes, until soft with a little crunch.

Add the spices–red chili, cumin powder, black pepper, and ½ the red pepper flakes. Keep stir-frying for 5 minutes, until aromatic. Set aside.

Heat the remaining 2 tablespoons oil in a separate pan over medium-high heat; then stir-fry potatoes for 5 minutes, until crispy golden. Add them to the sweet potato hash, and gently fold in, until they infuse all the other flavors–for about 2 minutes.

Sprinkle the remaining red chili flakes, and squeeze the lemon juice. Give a gentle mix, to incorporate all flavors; then transfer into a serving dish. Serve hot Shakarkandi Makai Hash as a side dish with any pasta dish.

Variations:
For *Crostini*, spread shakarkandi makai hash on a baguette slice with a little cheese on top. Broil for a minute, until cheese melts, then serve.

For *Grilled Hash Sandwich*, toast two bread slices, then spread 2 tablespoons of hash mix on one, and top it with the other. Melt little margarine or butter on a non-stick pan, then place the sandwich, and press with a wooden spatula, until golden and crispy on the underside. Flip over, and repeat; then cut diagonally, to make 2 triangle sandwiches.

Shakarkandi Makai Hash *(Sweet Potato Corn Hash)*

Chicken, Fish and Meat

Tandoori Chicken, Chicken Tikka Masala, Chicken Makhani, Coconut Fish, Grilled Fish, Keema Masala, and Rogan Josh, are some of the popular dishes around the world.

Being a vegetarian, it took me many years to get used to cooking non-vegetarian food. Now I enjoy making it, and want to learn to cook more chicken, fish and meat dishes. It will be so much fun to be able to do that; then share my recipes with you all!

Murg Makhani
(Butter Chicken)

Murg Makhani *(Butter Chicken)*

Murg Makhani is chicken cooked in butter with Indian spices, to give it a creamy and buttery taste; hence the name *butter chicken*. It is a classic Punjabi recipe, which was probably improved by the Punjabi people, during the Mughal Empire in 16th century, but its origin goes back to the Parsi *(Persian)* Era in 550 B.C.

Serves 4
Ingredients:

Prep Time: 20 minutes
Cooking Time: 1 hour 20 minutes
Inactive time: 12 hours

8 Skinless Chicken *(Murg)* Drum Sticks
2 big Cloves Garlic *(Lehsun)*–grated
1 tablespoon Minced Ginger and Green Chili *(Adrak-Hari Mirch)*
2 tablespoons Lemon Juice *(Neembu Rus)*
1 teaspoon Salt *(Namak)*
½ teaspoon Red Chili Powder *(Lal Mirch)*
1 teaspoon Roasted Cumin Powder *(Bhuna Zeera)*
½ teaspoon Mixed Spice *(Garam Masala)*
2 tablespoons Olive Oil *(Jaitoon Ka Tel)*

For Gravy

2 tablespoons Olive Oil *(Jaitoon Ka Tel)*
1 Large Onion *(Pyaz)*–finely chopped
2 big Cloves Garlic *(Lehsun)*–grated
½ teaspoon Minced Ginger and Green Chili *(Adrak-Hari Mirch)*
½ teaspoon Turmeric Powder *(Haldi)*
1 teaspoon Salt *(Namak)*
½ teaspoon Red Chili Powder *(Lal Mirch)*
2 teaspoons Coriander Powder *(Dhaniya)*
½ teaspoon Roasted Cumin Powder *(Bhuna Zeera)*
½ teaspoon Mixed Spice *(Garam Masala)*
1 large Tomato *(Timatar)*–finely chopped
½ cup Tomato Juice *(Timatar Rus)*
4 tablespoons Unsalted Butter *(Makkhan)*
2-3 drops Orange Food Color
2 teaspoons Dry Fenugreek Leaves *(Methi)*–soaked in ½ cup water
½ cup Heavy Cream
1 tablespoon Chopped Cilantro *(Hara Dhaniya)*–for garnish

Method:

To Marinate: Wash and pat dry the chicken drum sticks, then place them in a plastic container and refrigerate, until marinade is ready.

Combine garlic, ginger-green chili, lemon juice, salt, red chili, cumin powder, mixed spice, and oil, in a bowl, and mix well; then set aside for 10 minutes. Pour the marinade over chicken, then stir the pieces around, until coated well. Refrigerate overnight for 12 hours or more.

Preheat the oven at 425 degrees F. Shake off the extra marinade, and place the chicken on a sheet pan, lined with foil; on the middle rack.

Bake for 15 minutes, then turn off the oven and turn on the broiler. Place the rack 10 inch below the broiler. Roast the chicken under the broiler, for 5 minutes on each side, until it is lightly golden. Then, set aside to cool.

Butter Gravy: In a deep heavy base pot, heat oil over medium heat. Add onions, and sauté, for 6-8 minutes, until golden. Add garlic, and ginger-green chili, then cook for 1 minute.

Reduce the heat to low-medium, and add the dry spices–turmeric, salt, red chili, coriander, cumin powder, and mixed spice, then stir-fry for 1 minute. Add tomatoes, and tomato juice, then mix.

Cover and cook for 10 minutes, until tomatoes are soft, then turn off the heat. Uncover and allow it to cool for 10 minutes.

In an electric blender, puree the tomato mix, until smooth. Heat butter in the same pot, over low-medium heat, then transfer the puree into it. Add a few drops of orange food color, and mix to distribute it evenly.

Add the roasted chicken with its juices to the pot, and gently mix. Spoon out the soaked fenugreek leaves from the top, leaving the sand at the bottom. Then, add the leaves to the gravy, and mix again.

Cover and cook for 20 minutes, or until chicken is tender and curry is thick. Turn off the heat and leave it covered for 10 minutes, allowing the flavors to infuse together.

Spoon out the chicken into a serving dish, and add cream to the gravy, then mix. Pour the gravy over the chicken, and garnish with cilantro.

Serve hot Murg Makhani with fresh naan, kulcha, or zafrani chawal, accompanied with onion relish, mint yogurt sauce, and roasted papadam.

Variations:
-Substitute heavy cream with sour cream, for some tang.
-Add ½ cup blanched almond paste to the gravy, for additional richness.
-Add saffron to the gravy while cooking for additional flavor.
-Substitute chicken drumsticks with chicken breasts. Cut each into 3 pieces, then prepare the dish as in the recipe above.

Murg Tikka Masala
(Spicy Chicken Tikka)

Murg Tikka Masala is a popular dish from the Punjab region in India, called *spicy chicken tikka*. These are prepared from marinated chicken pieces, cooked in a tandoor, or baked and broiled in the oven; either way they are delicious. Adjust the spices according to your taste.

Serves 4

Ingredients:

For Marinade:

Prep Time: 20 minutes
Cooking Time: 50 minutes
Inactive Time: 12 hours

1 cup Plain Greek Yogurt *(Dahi)*
2 teaspoons Minced Ginger and Green Chili *(Adrak-Hari Mirch)*
2 big Cloves Garlic *(Lehsun)*–grated
1 teaspoon Mixed Spice *(Garam Masala)*
1 teaspoon Red Chili Powder *(Lal Mirch)*
1 tablespoon Lemon Juice *(Neembu Rus)*
1 tablespoon Vinegar *(Sirka)*
pinch of Saffron *(Zafran)*
2-3 drops of Orange Food Color
2 tablespoons Olive Oil *(Jaitoon Ka Tel)*

Also Needed:

4 boneless skinless Chicken Breasts *(Murg)*–cut into 2 inch pieces
1 tablespoon Olive Oil *(Jaitoon Ka Tel)*–for brushing

Method:

Combine all the above ingredients for the marinade in a bowl, and mix well. Place the chicken pieces in a medium plastic container; then pour the marinade over them.

Stir the pieces around with tongs, to coat them well with the marinade. Cover with the lid, and refrigerate overnight, or for at least 6 hours, if prepared and used on the same day.

Preheat the oven at 400 degrees F. Place the marinated chicken on a baking tray lined with foil and brushed with oil.

Pour half the marinade over the chicken, to keep it moist, and flavorful. Save the remaining for later. Place the tray on the middle rack in the oven, where it can get even heat, then bake for 20 minutes.

Turn the pieces over. Pour the remaining marinade on the chicken, then bake for another 20 minutes, until it cooks through. Turn off the oven.

Turn on the broiler. Then, place the chicken under the broiler, and broil for 5 minutes, until golden and charred.

Transfer Murg Tikka Masala on to a serving platter, and serve hot with onion relish, mint and tamarind chutney.

Variations:
-*Curry Chicken Tikka*–*Curry Murg Tikka:* Prepare the curry for chicken tikka by following the gravy recipe for chicken makhani, without the fenugreek leaves, and heavy cream. Add the grilled chicken pieces to the curry, and mix. Then, cover and allow cooking for 15 minutes over low-medium heat, until all flavors infuse together. Garnish with cilantro and serve hot Curry Chicken Tikka with naan, kulcha, or saffron rice, accompanied with onion relish and roasted papadam.

-*Pepper Mushroom Chicken Tikka:* Add colored diced bell peppers and mushrooms to the marinade, with the chicken, then thread them in to soaked wooden skewers, in alternate order. Bake, broil and eat.

Murg Tikka Masala *(Spicy Chicken Tikka)*

Tandoori Murg
(Tandoori Chicken)

Tandoori Murg originates from Punjab region in north India. Historically, a whole chicken was marinated, skewered, and roasted, in a *tandoor*–a clay oven. Then, fresh naan bread was made in the same tandoor, and served with the chicken. For this recipe, I have added a few new ingredients, and baked the chicken in the traditional oven, and it tastes Delicious!!

Serving: 5
Ingredients:
For Marinade:

Prep Time: 20 minutes
Cooking Time: 1 hour 10 minutes
Inactive Time: 12 hours

2 cups Plain Greek Yogurt *(Dahi)*
1 tablespoon Lemon Juice *(Neembu Rus)*
2 big Cloves Garlic *(Lehsun)*–grated
1 tablespoon Minced Ginger and Green Chili *(Adrak-Hari Mirch)*
2 teaspoons Salt *(Namak)*
2 teaspoons Red Chili Powder *(Lal Mirch)*
1 teaspoon Mixed Spice *(Garam Masala)*
1 teaspoon Turmeric Powder *(Haldi)*
2 teaspoons Crushed Black Pepper *(Kuti Kali Mirch)*
2 teaspoons Dry Basil
2 teaspoons Dry Oregano
2 tablespoons Teriyaki Sauce
4 tablespoons Plain Vinegar *(Sirka)*
2 drops Red, plus 2 drops Yellow Food Color
4 tablespoons Olive Oil *(Jaitoon Ka Tel)*

Also Needed:
5 boneless, skinless Chicken Breasts *(Murg)*–cut into 2 pieces each
1 tablespoon Melted Unsalted Butter *(Makkhan)*–for basting
1 tablespoon Chopped Cilantro *(Hara Dhaniya)*
1 tablespoon Melted Unsalted Butter *(Makkhan)*–for garnish

Method:

In a large bowl, combine together–yogurt, lemon juice, garlic, ginger-green chili, salt, red chili, mixed spice, turmeric, black pepper, basil, oregano, teriyaki sauce, vinegar, food color, and 3 tablespoons oil, to prepare the marinade.

Prick the chicken pieces with a fork, to allow the marinade to sink deep into the meat, and keep it moist and flavorful.

Add the chicken to the marinade, and coat well; then cover and refrigerate for 12 hours. The longer it marinates, the better it tastes.

Preheat the oven at 400 degrees F. Shake off the extra marinade, and place the chicken pieces on to a baking sheet lined with foil and brushed with oil. Place it in the oven on the middle rack, and bake for 30 minutes.

Meanwhile, cook the leftover marinade for 2 minutes over medium heat, until bubbly, stirring constantly. Turn the baking sheet around, so the chicken cooks evenly on all sides. Then, lightly baste the chicken with the cooked marinade. Bake it for another 30 minutes, until cooked through.

Reduce the oven temperature to 350 degrees F. Baste the chicken with melted butter; then place it back, this time on the bottom rack of the oven, for another 10 minutes, until sizzling, lightly charred and still moist.

Remove the chicken, and transfer on to a serving platter. Garnish with more melted butter, and cilantro, and serve hot Tandoori Murg with onion relish, and sautéed vegetables *(P150)*.

Variations:
-Add 2 tablespoons mint chutney to the marinade for extra flavor.
-Baste the chicken with tamarind chutney, half way through the baking process, for an additional sweet and tangy flavor.

Tandoori Murg *(Tandoori Chicken)*

Nariyal Machchi
(Coconut Fish Curry)

Nariyal Machchi is a traditional South Indian *coconut fish curry,* and it is prepared from cooking any white fish, in coconut milk. For this recipe, I have used Tilapia fish.

Serves 4
Ingredients:

Prep Time: 10 minutes
Cooking Time: 40 minutes

3 tablespoons Olive Oil *(Jaitoon Ka Tel)*
1 medium Onion *(Pyaz)*–finely chopped
1 big Clove Garlic *(Lehsun)*–grated
1 teaspoon Minced Ginger and Green Chili *(Adrak-Hari Mirch)*
1 teaspoon Mixed Spice *(Garam Masala)*
2 Bay Leaves *(Tej Patta)*
½ teaspoon Turmeric Powder *(Haldi)*
½ teaspoon Roasted Cumin Powder *(Bhuna Zeera)*
½ teaspoon Fresh Crushed Black Pepper *(Kuti Kali Mirch)*
1 teaspoon Salt *(Namak)*
1 tablespoon Lemon Juice *(Neembu Rus)*
1 Tomato *(Timatar)*–finely chopped
8 Tilapia Fish Fillets *(Machchi)*
1 cup Coconut Milk *(Nariyal Doodh)*
1 tablespoon Fresh Chopped Cilantro *(Hara Dhaniya)*–for garnish

Method:

Heat the oil in a non-stick skillet, over medium heat. Add onions and sauté for 5 minutes, until lightly golden. Add garlic, ginger-green chili, and mixed spice, then cook for a few minutes, until aromatic.

Reduce the heat to low-medium, and add bay leaves, turmeric, cumin powder, black pepper, salt, lemon juice, and tomatoes; then stir. Cover and cook for 10 minutes, until tomatoes are soft and mushy; and form a smooth sauce. Stir a few times. Reduce heat to low, and add fish. Gently shake the skillet, then cover and cook for 10 minutes, until tender.

Note: Don't touch the fish while cooking, because it breaks easily.

Reduce the heat further to simmer, and add the coconut milk, then gently shake the skillet again, without touching the fish. *Adding coconut milk on high heat makes it curdle.* Then, increase the heat to low.

Cook uncovered, for 10 minutes, or until the curry thickens. Garnish with cilantro, and serve hot Nariyal Machchi with zafrani chawal .

Nariyal Machchi
(Coconut Fish Curry)
Recipe on P145

Tandoori Machchi
(Broiled Fish)

Bhuni Machchi
(Grilled Fish)
Recipe on P148

Tandoori Machchi
(Broiled Fish)

Tandoori Machchi is a healthy *broiled fish*–an easy and quick recipe for a light lunch or dinner, and is prepared from Tilapia fish.

Serves 4
Ingredients:

Prep Time: 6 minutes
Cooking Time: 10 minutes

1 tablespoon Lemon Juice *(Neembu Rus)*
¼ teaspoon Garlic Powder
¼ teaspoon Onion Powder
¼ teaspoon Turmeric Powder *(Haldi)*
½ teaspoon Salt *(Namak)*
½ teaspoon Ground Black Pepper *(Pisi Kali Mirch)*
½ teaspoon Roasted Cumin Powder *(Bhuna Zeera)*
4 tablespoons Olive Oil *(Jaitoon Ka Tel)*–divided
8 Tilapia Fish Fillets *(Machchi)*
2 teaspoons Plain Bread Crumbs
4 teaspoons Teriyaki Sauce
2 Lemon Wedges
Also Needed: A Sheet Pan, Olive Oil Cooking Spray, A Brush

Method:
Prepare a sheet pan by spraying it with cooking spray, then set aside. Combine lemon juice, garlic powder, onion powder, turmeric, salt, black pepper, cumin powder, and 3 tablespoons of olive oil in a medium bowl, then whisk to make a smooth spice mix.

Place the fish fillets on the prepared sheet pan, in a single layer, and brush them well on both sides with the spice mix. Then, sprinkle the bread crumbs on top, and drizzle with the remaining oil.

Turn on the broiler (500 degrees F). Place the fish 10 inch below the broiler, and broil for 6-7 minutes, until lightly golden on top. Remove the fish with a flat spoon, and transfer it on to a serving platter.

Deglaze the sheet pan with teriyaki sauce, and mix with the fish juices. Then, cook this liquid in a small pan for a few minutes, until bubbly; forming a smooth sauce. Garnish the fish with the prepared sauce, and lemon wedges; then serve hot with crispy green beans *(P117)*.

Bhuni Machchi
(Grilled Fish)

Bhuni Machchi is a flavorful *grilled fish*, prepared and cooked in 25 minutes. For this recipe, I have used white Flounder fish.

Serves 2
Ingredients:
Prep Time: 15 minutes
Cooking Time: 10 minutes

1 tablespoon Olive Oil *(Jaitoon Ka Tel)*
2 White Flounder Fish Fillets *(Machchi)*

For Rub:
¼ teaspoon Paprika
¼ teaspoon Dry Basil
¼ teaspoon Dry Sage
¼ teaspoon Dry Rosemary
¼ teaspoon Onion Powder
¼ teaspoon Garlic Powder
¼ teaspoon Ginger Powder *(Pisa Adrak)*
1 teaspoon Coriander Powder *(Dhaniya)*
¼ teaspoon Turmeric Powder *(Haldi)*
¼ teaspoon Salt *(Namak)*
¼ teaspoon Ground Black Pepper *(Pisi Kali Mirch)*
2 teaspoons Lime Juice *(Neembu Rus)*
1 tablespoon Olive Oil *(Jaitoon Ka Tel)*

Garnish: 2 Lime *(Neembu)* quarters

Method:
Combine all the ingredients for the rub in a bowl, then mix, and set aside for 5 minutes. Meanwhile, pat dry the fish, and apply the rub evenly, on both sides, then refrigerate it for 10 minutes.

Heat a grill pan over medium heat, then brush it with a little oil. Place the fish on the pan, and grill it, for 5 minutes on each side, until golden. Remove, and transfer the fish, on to serving platter, then garnish with lime, and serve hot Bhuni Machchi with sautéed vegetables *(P150)*.

Variations:
-For *Grilled Fish Sandwich*–Bhuni Machchi Sandwich, take 2 ciabatta bread slices, and spread some butter on each, then grill on a hot grill pan. Place a fish fillet on one slice, and top it with the other. Lightly press it, then cut diagonally into two sandwiches. Serve hot.

Machchi Taco
(Fish Taco)

I always wanted to make Fish Tacos–they seemed so easy, so I decided to make them when my children were home for the holidays. I used Tilapia fish, flour tortillas, and my own concoction of spices. They turned out delicious. My son Swaraj helped me put this dish together.

Serves 2-3
Ingredients:

Prep Time: 20 minutes
Cooking Time: 50 minutes

5 Tilapia Fish Fillets *(Machchi)*
3 tablespoons Olive Oil *(Jaitoon Ka Tel)*
For Rub:
1 teaspoon Salt *(Namak)*
1 teaspoon Fresh Crushed Black Pepper *(Kuti Kali Mirch)*
1 teaspoon Garlic Powder
1 teaspoon Onion Powder
1 teaspoon Paprika
½ teaspoon Dry Oregano
½ teaspoon Dry Thyme
1 teaspoon Chopped Cilantro *(Hara Dhaniya)*
For Pico-De-Gallo (Salsa):
2 medium Tomatoes *(Timatar)*–chopped
¼ Onion *(Pyaz)*–chopped
1 teaspoon Lemon Zest
1 teaspoon Fresh Chopped Cilantro *(Hara Dhaniya)*
Dash of Salt, Black Pepper, Crushed Red Pepper and Lemon Juice
For Sautéed Vegetables:
1 tablespoon Olive Oil *(Jaitoon Ka Tel)*
¼ Onion *(Pyaz)*–chopped
5 Colored Mini Sweet Peppers *(Choti Shimla Mirch)*–julienned
Dash of Salt, Black Pepper and Lemon Juice

Method:
Combine all the ingredients for the rub in a bowl, then mix, and apply on each fillet, in the direction of the scales on the fish, until nicely coated. Set aside for 5 minutes.

Meanwhile, combine the ingredients for the *Pico-De-Gallo* in another bowl without the lemon juice, and mix. Cover, and set aside.

Sauté Vegetables: Heat the oil in a non-stick skillet over medium heat. Add onions, and sauté, for about 5 minutes, until lightly golden.

Add julienned peppers, salt, and black pepper, and sauté for 2 more minutes, until tender, but still crunchy.

Squeeze a dash of lemon juice, then turn off the heat. Transfer the sautéed peppers into another bowl, and set them aside to use later.

Sear Fish: In the same skillet, heat more oil over medium heat, then pan sear 3 fish fillets, for 5 minutes, on each side, until golden.

Remove, and transfer the seared fish on to a plate. Repeat the process with the remaining fish fillets, until all are cooked.

Assemble Fish Taco: Warm up tortillas in the same skillet, one at a time, over low heat, for 30 seconds on each side, until all are done. Cover them with a foil to keep warm, and start assembling the fish taco.

Place one tortilla on a plate; then place one fish fillet on it, on one side. Top it with sautéed vegetables, then garnish with some pico-de-gallo, without the liquid, and a dash of lemon juice.

Fold the other side of tortilla over the fish; then place it on a serving platter. Repeat the process to assemble the remaining tacos. Serve Machchi Taco with mint chutney.

Variations:
-Substitute the fish with grilled chicken to make chicken tacos.

-Substitute the fish with keema masala to make meat tacos.

-Substitute fish with sautéed potatoes and mini peppers to make vegetarian tacos.

Seared Machchi *(Pan Seared Fish)*

Open Machchi Taco *(Open Fish Taco)*

Folded Machchi Taco *(Folded Fish Taco)*

Keema Masala
(Spicy Minced Meat Curry)

Keema Masala is a traditional South Asian dish, called *spicy minced meat curry*. It can be prepared from any mincemeat, such as: lamb, beef, or turkey, then cooked with peas, for additional flavor.

Serves 4 *Prep Time: 10 minutes*
Ingredients: *Cooking Time: 40 minutes*
3 tablespoons Olive Oil *(Jaitoon Ka Tel)*
½ teaspoon Cumin Seeds *(Zeera)*
2 medium Onions *(Pyaz)*–finely chopped
3 big Cloves Garlic *(Lehsun)*–grated
1 tablespoon Minced Ginger and Green Chili *(Adrak-Hari Mirch)*
½ pound Ground Turkey
½ teaspoon Turmeric Powder *(Haldi)*
2 teaspoons Coriander Powder *(Dhaniya)*
1 teaspoon Roasted Cumin Powder *(Bhuna Zeera)*
½ teaspoon Red Chili Powder *(Lal Mirch)*
1 teaspoon Salt *(Namak)*
½ cup Plain Greek Yogurt *(Dahi)*
1 cup Green Peas *(Hari Matar)*–fresh or frozen
½ teaspoon Mixed Spice *(Garam Masala)*
1 tablespoons Chopped Cilantro *(Hara Dhaniya)*–for garnish

Method:
Heat the oil in a medium saucepan, over medium heat. Add cumin seeds, and allow them to crackle. Add onions, and sauté, for about 5 minutes, until lightly golden. Add garlic, and ginger-green chili, then cook for 1 minute, until fragrant.

Reduce the heat to low-medium. Add ground turkey with dry spices; turmeric, coriander, cumin powder, red chili, and salt. Then, cook for 15 minutes, until meat is brown; stirring often, to prevent burning.

Add yogurt, peas, and mixed spice, then mix everything well. Cover and cook for another 20 minutes, until meat has cooked through, and infused with the various flavors. Stir a few times in between.

Garnish with cilantro, and serve hot Keema Masala with fresh roti, or parantha, accompanied with onion relish and mint chutney.

Variations:

-Use keema masala as a stuffing for samosa, or kulcha.

-*Spicy Meat Sauce:* Cook the sauce with 1 cup each tomato puree and vegetable juice; 2 tablespoons oil, plus spices to taste, over low-medium heat, for 15 minutes, until thick, and oil separates. Mix in keema masala, and cook for 15 minutes. Serve hot with plain pasta, or use in lasagna.

Keema Masala *(Spicy Minced Meat Curry)*

Meat Kofta *Curry (Meat Ball Curry) Recipe on P154*

Meat Kofta Curry
(Meat Balls Curry)

Meat Kofta Curry; also called *meat balls curry*, is a famous comfort food. Meat balls, can be prepared using any mincemeat, such as: beef, turkey, or lamb, and then cooked in tomato and onion sauce. For this recipe, I have used ground turkey; it is lighter and healthier.

Serves 6　　　　　　　　　　　*Prep Time: 30 minutes*
Ingredients:　　　　　　　　*Cooking Time: 1 hour 40 minutes*

For Meat Balls: Makes 12
3 tablespoons Olive Oil *(Jaitoon Ka Tel)*–divided
2 big Cloves Garlic *(Lehsun)*–grated
1 teaspoon Minced Ginger and Green Chili *(Adrak-Hari Mirch)*
1 teaspoon Salt *(Namak)*
½ teaspoon Crushed Black Pepper *(Kuti Kali Mirch)*
½ teaspoon Roasted Cumin Powder *(Bhuna Zeera)*
½ teaspoon Mixed Spice *(Garam Masala)*
¼ teaspoon Sugar *(Chini)*
½ cup Plain Greek Yogurt *(Dahi)*
1 Egg–beaten
1 pound Ground Turkey

For Curry
1 tablespoon Olive Oil *(Jaitoon Ka Tel)*
1 tablespoon Unsalted Butter *(Makkhan)*
1 large Onion *(Pyaz)*–minced
2 big Cloves Garlic *(Lehsun)*–grated
1 teaspoon Minced Ginger and Green Chili *(Adrak-Hari Mirch)*
½ teaspoon Turmeric Powder *(Haldi)*
1 tablespoon Coriander Powder *(Dhaniya)*
½ teaspoon Red Chili Powder *(Lal Mirch)*
½ teaspoon Salt *(Namak)*
½ teaspoon Roasted Cumin Powder *(Bhuna Zeera)*
½ teaspoon Mixed Spice *(Garam Masala)*
1 large Tomato *(Timatar)*–minced
1 cup Tomato Juice *(Timatar Rus)*
pinch of Saffron *(Zafran)*
1 cup Hot Tap Water (reduces cooking time)
1 tablespoon Chopped Cilantro *(Hara Dhaniya)*–for garnish

Method:
For Meat Balls–*Meat Koftas*; combine 1 tablespoon oil, garlic, ginger-green chili, salt, black pepper, cumin, mixed spice, sugar, and yogurt, in a medium bowl, then mix. Check the seasoning; then add egg, and the ground meat. Lightly mix with a fork without over working the meat, as it will result into hard meat balls. Cover and refrigerate for 15 minutes.

Divide the mix into 12 equal portions, then roll each between your palms into a round ball. Place them on a greased baking sheet, and drizzle the remaining oil on top. Bake in a preheated oven at 350 degrees F, for 25-30 minutes, until lightly golden on all sides. Remove and set them aside.

For Curry; heat the oil in a wide deep pan, over medium heat, then add butter, and allow it to melt. Add onions, and sauté, for 5 minutes, until lightly golden. Then, add garlic and ginger-green chili, and sauté for 1 minute, until fragrant.

Reduce the heat to low, and add turmeric, coriander, red chili, salt, cumin powder, and mixed spice, then sauté for a minute.

Add tomatoes, and tomato juice, then mix well. Increase the heat to low-medium, then cover, and cook for 15 minutes, until tomatoes are soft, and mushy; the sauce is thicker, and the oil separates. Stir in between.

Add saffron and water, then mix. Increase the heat to medium, until the curry comes to a boil. Add the meat balls, and stir gently. Cover and cook for 5 minutes, until they puff up.

Reduce the heat to low-medium, and continue to cook covered, for another 10 minutes, until meat balls are almost double in size. Gently stir once in between. Partially cover, and cook for 10 more minutes, until the gravy is thick; the meat balls are soft, and cooked through.

To *serve*; spoon out the meat balls into a serving dish, then pour the curry over them evenly. Garnish with cilantro, and serve hot Meat Kofta Curry, with naan or kulcha, accompanied with onion relish.

Variations:
-Serve just meat balls without the gravy; and with mint chutney.
-Add meat balls with a little gravy into a hot dog bun. Top it with caramelized onions, and crispy bacon, then serve.

Rogan Josh
(Lamb Curry)

Rogan Josh is an aromatic *lamb curry*, originating from the Mughal Empire era, around the 15th century, and since then, it has been dominant in Kashmir, in the northern part of India.

The history behind this dish is that the harsh heat of the Indian plains made Mughals frequently visit Kashmir and that's how it was adopted by *Kashmiris*–the people of Kashmir. 'Rogan' means *Oil*, while 'Josh' means *Intense Heat* — thus meaning–cooked in oil, at intense heat.

Kashmiri dishes are butter based, and use both ground and whole spices, to bring a very distinguished flavor. I grind all the spices, then cook the dish in oil, and add a little butter on top for the garnish. It is a low fat dish, yet full of flavor and aroma.

Serves 2 *Prep Time: 15 minutes*
Ingredients: *Cooking Time: 1 hour 40 minutes*

4 tablespoons Olive Oil *(Jaitoon Ka Tel)*
½ pound Leg of Lamb–cubed
1 teaspoon Cumin Seeds *(Zeera)*
2 medium Onions *(Pyaz)*–minced
3 big Cloves Garlic *(Lehsun)*–grated
1 Bay Leaf *(Tej Patta)*
2 teaspoons Minced Ginger and Green Chili *(Adrak-Hari Mirch)*
½ teaspoon Turmeric Powder *(Haldi)*
1 teaspoon Salt *(Namak)*–add more as needed
2 teaspoons Coriander Powder *(Dhaniya)*
½ teaspoon Red Chili Powder *(Lal Mirch)*
½ teaspoon Ground Black Pepper *(Kali Mirch)*
1 tablespoon Mixed Spice *(Garam Masala)*–divided
6 tablespoons Plain Greek Yogurt *(Dahi)*
2 cups Hot Tap Water (reduces cooking time)
1 tablespoon Unsalted Butter *(Makkhan)*
1 tablespoon Chopped Cilantro *(Hara Dhaniya)*–for garnish

Also Needed:
Medium Heavy Base Pot–for cooking
Wooden Spoon

Method:
Heat oil in the pot, over medium-high heat, and add lamb cubes, then stir-fry for 10 minutes, until brown on all sides–stirring constantly. Reduce the heat to low-medium, then remove the meat pieces with a slotted spoon, into a bowl, and set aside.

Increase the heat to medium, then add cumin seeds, and let them crackle. Add onions, and sauté for 6-8 minutes, until golden, and the oil separates.

Reduce the heat to low-medium, and add garlic, bay leaf, ginger-green chili, and the dry spices–turmeric, salt, coriander, red chili, black pepper, and half the mixed spice. Stir-fry for 1 minute, until aromatic.

Add the meat back with its juices, then mix well. Cover and cook for 10 minutes, until it turns more golden brown. Stir often. Increase the heat to medium, and add yogurt, 1 tablespoon at a time; mixing and stirring constantly, until it completely blends with the spices; for about 5 minutes.

Add water, and stir well, then cover and cook for 45 minutes over low-medium heat, until the meat is tender; the gravy begins to thicken, and the oil separates. Add butter, then mix again.

Partially cover, and cook for another 15 minutes over low-medium heat, until gravy is thick. Turn off the heat, and sprinkle the remaining mixed spice on top, then cover for 5 minutes, to infuse all the flavors.

Note: Spoon out some of the fat, or leave it in for extra flavor.

Transfer the curry into a serving dish, then garnish with cilantro. Serve hot Rogan Josh with naan, kulcha, or plain rice, accompanied with onion relish, and mint chutney.

Variations:
Add:
-2 tablespoons fresh fenugreek leaves to the gravy; while cooking.
-1 cup fresh spinach to the gravy; while cooking.
-¼ cup heavy cream to the gravy, before serving; for extra flavor.
-½ cup tomato puree, before adding the yogurt, and cook as in the recipe.
-1 tablespoon mint chutney to the gravy for some extra flavor.

COOK THE INDIAN WAY

Rogan Josh *(Lamb Curry) Recipe on P156*

Murg Pie *(Chicken Pie)*

158

Easy Steps to Everyday Cooking

Murg Pie
(Chicken Pie)

Murg Pie is a delicious and healthy *chicken pie*–a complete meal in itself; with proteins, carbohydrates, and fiber, from meat, crust, and vegetables, respectively–a perfect balance! To prepare the chicken pie for this recipe, I have used two 9 by 9 by 2 inch size, round pie molds.

Serves 8, Makes 2 Round Pies
Ingredients:
For Rub:

Prep Time: 20 minutes
Cooking Time: 1 hour 15 minutes
Inactive Time: 1 hour

2 big Cloves Garlic *(Lehsun)*–grated
1 teaspoon Salt *(Namak)*
½ teaspoon Ground Black Pepper *(Pisi Kali Mirch)*
1 teaspoon Dry Basil
1 tablespoon Olive Oil *(Jaitoon Ka Tel)*

Also Needed:
2-3 Boneless-Skinless Chicken Breasts *(Murg)*
4 Sheets Pie Crusts–store bought

For Gravy:
3 tablespoons Unsalted Butter *(Makkhan)*–divided
2 tablespoons Olive Oil *(Jaitoon Ka Tel)*–divided
2 big Cloves Garlic *(Lehsun)*–grated
½ cup washed, peeled and Finely Chopped Celery
½ cup washed, cleaned and Finely Chopped Leeks
½ cup cleaned and Chopped Button Mushrooms *(Khumbi)*
1/3 cup frozen and thawed Green Peas *(Hari Matar)*
1½ tablespoons All-Purpose Flour *(Maida)*
1/3 cup 2% Milk *(Doodh)*
1 cup Chicken Stock
½ teaspoon Salt *(Namak)*
½ teaspoon Ground Black Pepper *(Pisi Kali Mirch)*
1 teaspoon Ground Nutmeg *(Pisa Jaiphal)*

For Egg Wash: 1 beaten Egg, plus 1 tablespoon Water mixed

Method:

Combine garlic, salt, pepper, basil, and oil, in a bowl, then mix, and rub on the chicken. Cover, and refrigerate for 15 minutes. Preheat the oven at 350 degrees F, and place the chicken on a baking sheet lined with foil, to prevent juices from overflowing and burning. Bake for 25-30 minutes, until golden and cooked through. Check by inserting a toothpick. Remove, and allow cooling, for 15 minutes, then cut into small cubes, and set aside.

In a medium pot, heat 1 tablespoon each butter and oil, over low-medium heat; then add garlic, celery, leeks, mushrooms, and peas; and mix well. Cover and cook for 10 minutes, until vegetables are tender. Remove, and transfer into a bowl, then set aside.

In the same pot, add the remaining butter, and allow it to melt. Then, add the flour, and whisk, for 2-3 minutes, until it is bubbly, and cooks through, but is not brown.

Add milk, then the chicken stock, while whisking constantly, until smooth, without any lumps. Increase the heat to medium-high, and continue to stir, until the liquid comes to a boil. Reduce the heat to low-medium, then stir and cook, for 10 minutes, until the gravy is thick.

Add salt, pepper, nutmeg, chicken, and vegetables, to the gravy, then gently mix, to combine everything well. Set aside to cool for 15 minutes.

Meanwhile, take out the pie crusts from the freezer and leave them out for 15 minutes to defrost. Grease the two round pie pans, with the remaining oil, then roll out two pie crusts, and place them in each pan, being sure to cover the base, sides, and edges. Cut the extra overhanging crust with a knife or kitchen scissors for neatness.

Distribute the chicken mix evenly into the two pans. Then, brush the edges of the crust with egg wash, and cover with the other round pieces of the crusts as the lids. With a fork, firmly press the edges of the crust together, so it is secured and doesn't open while baking.

Brush the top lightly with egg wash for a crispy golden crust. Make 3 small slits on the top of each pie, to release steam while baking.

Place both pies on a baking sheet, making it easy to remove them later, and also collect any gravy that may overflow.

Bake at 350 degrees F, for 25-30 minutes, or until crispy golden. Remove, and let them cool for 10 minutes, cut into slices, and serve hot.

Variations:
-Bake double crusted individual small pies, in molds that are 3 cm deep, 7.5 cm across the base and 12.5 cm across the top. This recipe will make 4 individual sized pies.

Cornish Pasty
(Meat Pie)

Cornish Pasty is an individual baked *meat pie*, stuffed with seasoned raw meat, and vegetable mix. This way each person gets his or her own pie. One pasty can also be stuffed with 2 different fillings–savory and sweet. The origin of the cornish pasty goes back to the 13th century, and comes from Cornwall, during the reign of Henry III. For this recipe, I have first cooked the filling, then stuffed it in the pastry, and baked it.

Serves 8, Makes 8
Ingredients:
For Pastry:

Prep Time: 45 minutes
Cooking Time: 1 hour 25 minutes
Inactive Time: 2 hours 20 minutes

4 cups All-Purpose Flour *(Maida)*
½ teaspoon Salt *(Namak)*
1½ cups Cold Unsalted Butter *(Makkhan)*–cut into ¼ inch cubes
12 tablespoons Iced Water

For Filling:
3 tablespoons Olive Oil *(Jaitoon Ka Tel)*
1 big Onion *(Pyaz)*–chopped
½ cup Washed and Chopped Celery
2 medium Potatoes *(Aloo)*–half boiled, peeled and cubed
½ cup Green Peas *(Hari Matar)*–frozen or fresh
2 cups Cubed Lean Boneless Beef
1½ teaspoons Salt *(Namak)*
1 teaspoon Ground Black Pepper *(Pisi Kali Mirch)*
½ teaspoon Ginger Powder *(Pisa Adrak)*
½ teaspoon Roasted Cumin Powder *(Bhuna Zeera)*
2 cups Beef Stock

For Egg Wash: 1 beaten Egg, plus 1 tablespoon Water, mixed
Also Needed: Medium Heavy base Pot

Method:
For Pastry, mix flour, salt, and butter, in a food processor, or rub by hand, to make a coarse meal, until butter turns into the size of a pea. Add iced water, 1 tablespoon at a time, and knead to make firm dough.

If the dough doesn't bind, or crumbles, add a little more cold water. Then, wrap it in a plastic wrap, and refrigerate for 2 hours, to make it smooth and easy to roll.

For Filling, heat the oil over medium heat, then add onions, and sauté, for 5 minutes, until lightly golden. Add celery, potatoes, and peas, then sauté for another 2 minutes. Add meat, salt, black pepper, ginger powder, cumin powder, and beef stock, then mix well.

Allow the beef stock to boil, then reduce the heat to low-medium; cover and cook for 20-25 minutes, until the meat is tender, and vegetables are soft, with thick gravy. Remove from heat, and set aside to cool completely.

To Assemble Pasties, roll out the dough with a rolling pin, into a big circle, ¼ inch thick; then cut 6 rounds from it, using saucer as your guide. Take the remaining scraps of dough, then knead and roll again, to make some additional rounds.

In the center of each round, spoon 3 tablespoons of filling; leaving enough space on the sides, to fold and seal it. Brush a little egg wash on the pastry edges, then fold it over the filling, wrapping it inside, and sealing well. With a fork, press the edges of the pastry to secure them, preventing them from opening, and the filling oozing out, while baking.

Place all pasties on a baking sheet lined with wax paper. Brush lightly with egg wash and make two slits on top of each, to let steam escape.

Bake at 400 degrees F, for 20 minutes. Reduce the heat to 350 degrees F, and bake for another 30 minutes, until golden. Serve hot from the oven.

Cornish Pasty *(Meat Pie)*

Sausage Roll
(Meat Roll)

Sausage Roll is a delicious *meat roll*, originating from Italy. It is prepared from puff pastry, stuffed with sausage meat. I used to have these baked daily at my bakery in Botswana, Africa; and everyone loved them.

Serves 8, Makes: 8
Ingredients:

Prep Time: 30 minutes
Cooking Time: 30 minutes
Inactive Time: 15 minutes

2 Sheets of Puff Pastry–store bought
1 tablespoon Olive Oil *(Jaitoon Ka Tel)*
1 Onion *(Pyaz)*–finely chopped
2 big Cloves Garlic *(Lehsun)*–grated
1 tablespoon Fresh Basil Leaves or ½ teaspoon dry Basil
½ teaspoon Dry Oregano
½ teaspoon Salt *(Namak)*
½ teaspoon Ground Black Pepper *(Pisi Kali Mirch)*
½ teaspoon Nutmeg Powder *(Pisa Jaiphal)*
½ cup Plain Bread Crumbs
1 tablespoon Fresh Chopped Cilantro *(Hara Dhaniya)*
1 pound Pork Sausage
For Egg Wash: 1 beaten Egg, plus 1 tablespoon Water, mixed

Method:
Leave the pastry out of the freezer, for 15 minutes, to thaw. Meanwhile heat the oil in a medium pan, over medium heat. Add onions, and sauté, for 3 minutes, until translucent, then add garlic, basil, and oregano. Cook for one minute, then set aside to cool.

For filling, combine salt, black pepper, nutmeg, bread crumbs, cilantro, pork sausage, and onion mix, in a medium bowl; then with clean hands, scrunch, to mix all the ingredients evenly. Set aside, and wash hands.

Dust your work surface with dry flour, then with a rolling pin, roll each pastry sheet into a 12 by 12 inch square. Cut from the center, into two long even rectangles. Spoon the sausage mix along the long edge of the pastry away from you, leaving little space to put the egg wash; then use your hands to make into an even sausage shape.

Lightly brush all the edges of the pastry with egg wash, then roll the edge closer to you, over the filling, wrapping it inside. Press down the edges with your fingers, then seal the joint with a fork.

Cut the rolls, into the size you want, and space them out on the baking tray lined with wax paper.

Brush the top of each sausage roll with egg wash, and bake in a preheated oven at 350 degrees F, for 25 minutes, or until puffed golden, and cooked through. Serve hot from the oven.

Sausage Roll *(Meat Roll) Recipe on P163*

Murg Pie Slice *(Chicken Pie Slice) Recipe on P159*

Indian Breads

Indian Breads are delicious and easy to make, and are popular around the world. People know what they are, and make them in their homes and restaurants every day.

Plain Tava Roti is whole wheat flatbread, roasted over a hot griddle, and is part of Indian staple food; eaten daily. Tava roti is served with dal–*lentil soup*, subzi–*vegetable curry*, or meat curry, accompanied with plain yogurt, or yogurt raita.

Besides tava roti, Plain or Stuffed Parantha–*pan fried flatbread,* are also among the staple foods in India, and are eaten for breakfast, lunch or dinner.

The popular breads for special occasions, and festivals are: Poori–*deep fried puffed wheat bread*, Bhatura–*deep fried puffed white bread*, and Naan–*tandoor or oven baked white flatbread*.

Freshly prepared breads, available daily in restaurants are: Naan, Bhatura, Plain or Stuffed Kulcha–*griddle roasted white flatbread*, and Tandoori Roti–*tandoor roasted wheat flatbread*.

Plain Parantha *(Plain Pan Fried Flatbread) Recipe on P172*

Tava Roti
(Griddle Roasted Wheat Flatbread)

Tava Roti is a healthy, whole wheat flatbread, also called *chapatti*, and is very easy to make. It is prepared from stoneground whole meal roti flour–*atta or chapatti flour* that originated, and is consumed daily, in India, Pakistan, Nepal, Sri Lanka and Bangladesh.

Serves 2-3, Makes 6
Ingredients:
1½ cups Roti Wheat Flour *(Atta)*–divided
¼ cup Water
1 teaspoon Vegetable Oil
1 tablespoon Margarine, or Unsalted Butter for brushing
Also Needed: Cast Iron Griddle *(Tava)*, Kitchen Tongs

Prep Time: 10 minutes
Cooking Time: 20 minutes
Inactive Time: 25 minutes

Method:
Take 1 cup flour in a medium bowl, and add water slowly, while kneading, to make soft pliable dough, for about 5 minutes. Apply little oil, then cover with a plastic wrap and refrigerate for 20 minutes.

Note: Rested dough helps make soft and fluffy roti, otherwise it will be flat, tough, and dry to eat.

Divide the dough into 6 equal portions, then roll and lightly press each, to make flat round discs. Cover them with a damp paper towel, to prevent drying, and let them rest for 5 more minutes.

Meanwhile, heat the griddle, over medium heat. Lightly flour the surface, then with a rolling pin, roll out one disc, into a 5 inch round, making the edges slightly thinner than the center part.

While rolling the roti, turn, and dust lightly with dry flour, 2-3 times, to prevent the dough from sticking to the surface, or the rolling pin. Keep the other discs covered, to prevent drying.

Lift the rolled roti, and flip between your hands a couple of times, then place it on the griddle. You can also place it without flipping; making sure it is not wrinkled, when placed on the griddle.

Wait for a minute, until roti changes color, to one shade darker, and little bubbles appear on top. Reduce the heat to low-medium, then flip it over with kitchen tongs, and cook the other side, for 30 seconds. Once both sides are lightly cooked, remove it from the griddle with tongs

On a Gas Burner: Place it over a low-medium flame, and it will puff up immediately. Use tongs to flip quickly, and roast the other side. Repeat a few times, until lightly golden on both sides, and edges cook as well.

On an Electric Burner: Puff up the roti on the griddle, over medium heat, by gently pressing its edges with a flat spoon, making sure not to burst it. Keep flipping and pressing a few times, until lightly golden on both sides. Remove and brush roti with a little margarine or butter, and serve hot. Adjust heat between low-medium and medium, as needed.

For a later eating time; cool, and wrap the rotis' in foil, and place in a 200 degrees F oven, to keep them warm, until the serving time.

Variations:
-Make *Tandoor Roasted Flatbread*–*Tandoori Roti,* by adding 2 tablespoons plain yogurt, ½ teaspoon baking soda, to the wheat flour. Knead with warm water, to make soft dough. Cover, and leave in a warm place for 2 hours, to rise and ferment. Roll 3 rotis at a time, place on a baking tray, and roast under the broiler for a minute on each side. Brush with melted butter, and serve hot.

Tava Roti *(Griddle Roasted Wheat Flatbread)*

Bhatura
(Fried Puffed Bread)

Bhatura is *fried puffed bread*, prepared from all-purpose flour, and semolina dough; then rolled and deep fried. Bhatura, accompanied with masala choley, is a popular food combination in north India, and it originates from the Punjab region. I used to eat choley bhaturey, almost daily in my college days, with onion rings and mango pickle. Yum!!

Serves 8, Makes 18
Ingredients:

Prep Time: 20 minutes
Cooking Time: 40 minutes
Inactive Time: 12 hours 10 minutes

3 cups All-Purpose Flour *(Maida)*
1 cup Semolina *(Sooji)*
1 teaspoon Baking Soda
1 teaspoon Salt *(Namak)*
1 cup Plain Greek Yogurt *(Dahi)*
1/3 cup Vegetable Oil
1 cup Warm Water
½ cup All-Purpose Flour *(Maida)*–for rolling
2 cups Vegetable Oil–for frying

Method:
Combine flour, semolina, baking soda, and salt, in a large deep bowl. Make a well in the center of the flour, then add yogurt and oil, and mix well, to distribute everything evenly.

Add warm water slowly, and knead, until just combined, to make a soft dough. Add a little more water as needed.

Cover with a plastic wrap, and keep in a warm place overnight, or at least for 4-5 hours, if temperature is warm, until double in volume.

Punch and knead the dough again, to release all air. Divide it into 18 equal portions, then roll and press each, to make round flat discs. Cover with a damp paper towel, for about 10 minutes, until they rise again.

Heat the oil in a wok or karahi–*Indian wok,* over medium heat. Then, check the oil by sliding a small piece of dough in it, which should sizzle and rise to the top in 30 seconds, and not turn brown.

Take one disc, and dust with some dry flour, then roll it with a rolling pin, into an 8 inch round *(it shrinks back an inch while frying).*

Carefully slide one bhatura in the oil from the side, then press in the center with a slotted spoon, to make it puff up like a ball. Fry for 1 minute, until lightly golden on the underside, then flip over, and fry for another minute, until lightly golden on the other side.

Note: Don't flip bhatura back and forth several times, as it soaks up too much oil. Adjust the heat between medium and low-medium temperatures, as needed.

Remove the bhatura with a slotted spoon, and transfer it on to a plate lined with a paper towel to drain excess oil. Repeat, until all bhaturas are fried. Serve hot with masala choley or any other curry.

If serving bhaturas at a later time, allow them to cool. Wrap them in foil, then place in a warm oven at 200 degrees F, until serving time.

Variations:
-For *Stuffed Puffed Bread*–*Bhurma Bhatura,* prepare the stuffing as in the recipe for aloo parantha *(P170),* with added ¼ cup cooked peas. Stuff 1 teaspoon filling in each dough disc, then close and seal securely. Cover and set aside for 5 minutes. Dust each disc with dry flour, then gently roll with a rolling pin, seal side up, to 6 by 6 inch round. Fry for 2 minutes on each side, until puffed and lightly golden. Remove and serve hot. Adjust spices to taste.

Bhatura *(Fried Puffed Bread)*

Aloo Parantha
(Potato Stuffed Flatbread)

Aloo Parantha is a popular Sunday brunch recipe in North India. It is a stuffed wheat flatbread, prepared from stuffing the potato mix in the dough balls, then rolled and pan fried. There are different fillings used to prepare stuffed parantha, but aloo parantha is the most popular one.

Serves 3, Makes 6
Ingredients:
For Dough:

Prep Time: 30 minutes
Cooking Time: 35 minutes
Inactive Time: 40 minutes

1 cup Roti Wheat Flour *(Atta)*
pinch of Salt *(Namak)* or to taste
1 tablespoon, plus 1 teaspoon Vegetable Oil
½ cup Water

For Stuffing:
2 medium Potatoes *(Aloo)*–washed and well-scrubbed
1 cup Hot Tap Water (reduces cooking time)
¼ teaspoon Salt *(Namak)*–add more as needed
½ teaspoon Roasted Cumin Powder *(Bhuna Zeera)*
½ teaspoon Red Chili Powder *(Lal Mirch)*
½ teaspoon Minced Green Chili *(Hari Mirch)* (Optional)
½ teaspoon Ginger Powder *(Pisa Adrak)*
1 tablespoon Chopped Cilantro *(Hara Dhaniya)*

For Cooking:
¼ cup Roti Wheat Flour *(Atta)*–for rolling
½ cup Vegetable Oil–for pan frying

Method:
For *dough*; combine flour, salt, and 1 tablespoon oil, in a medium bowl, or in a food processor. Then, add water a little at a time while kneading until a soft, smooth, and pliable dough forms; about 5 minutes. Apply 1 teaspoon oil on the dough, then place it in a plastic container and cover. Refrigerate for 20 minutes, for easy rolling.

Meanwhile, for *stuffing*, prick the potatoes with a fork a couple of times, then boil in the microwave, using 1 cup of hot tap water, for 8 minutes, or in a pot, using 2 cups of hot tap water, and covered, on the stove top, over low-medium heat, for 12-15 minutes, until they are soft. Check with a toothpick–it should go right through.

Drain the potatoes in a colander and set aside, for 10 minutes, until cool enough to handle *(don't cool under tap water)*. Remove the skin, then mash them with a potato masher, or a wooden spoon, until smooth.

Add salt, cumin powder, red chili, green chili, ginger, and cilantro, then gently mix to make soft potato dough. Cover and set aside for 5 minutes.

Cooking Potato Flatbread: Divide both the dough and stuffing, into 6 equal portions. Roll each portion between your palms, to make round balls, then lightly press each dough ball to make a flat disc.

Dip one dough disc in dry flour, and roll it with a rolling pin, into a 4 inch round. Place one portion of the stuffing in the center of the round.

Gently pull the edges of the round towards the center, wrapping the filling inside. Press, to seal in the center, making a stuffed flat disc.

Repeat, and finish stuffing the remaining discs. Cover with a damp paper towel, and allow them to rest for 5 minutes. Resting prevents the stuffing from bursting out while rolling.

Turn on the griddle, or a non-stick pan, to medium heat, and wait for a minute. Meanwhile, dip one stuffed disc in dry flour, then gently roll, with a rolling pin, sealed side up, into a 6 inch round.

Use dry flour a couple of times, to prevent dough from sticking to the rolling pin, or the surface.

Carefully lift the rolled flatbread, and flip it once between your hands, then place it on the hot griddle. Leave the flatbread for a minute, until it changes color to one shade darker.

Flip over the flatbread with a spatula, and it should have some light golden brown spots on top.

Wait for 30 seconds, then spread a teaspoon of oil on the flatbread. Flip it over and spread a teaspoon of oil on the other side.

Pan fry the flatbread for 1-2 minutes on each side, by gently pressing its edges and center with a wooden spatula, until golden and crispy on both sides. Then, reduce the heat to low-medium.

Transfer the flatbread on to a paper towel to drain excess oil. Repeat, until remaining stuffed flatbreads are cooked. Serve hot Aloo Parantha with cucumber yogurt sauce, onion relish, and tomato chutney.

For a later serving time, allow the flatbreads to cool, then wrap them in foil, and place in a 200 degrees F oven, to keep them warm, until the serving time.

Note: Adjust the cooking temperatures, between low-medium, and medium, as you need to accordingly, while cooking.

Variations:
-*Plain Pan Fried Flatbread*–*Plain Parantha:* Roll a plain dough disc, without the stuffing, into a 2 inch round, then spread a little oil on it. Fold the round in half, then again in half, making a triangle. Dip it in dry flour, and roll into a 6 inch triangle, then pan fry as in the recipe above.

-*Cauliflower Stuffed Flatbread*–*Gobhi Parantha:* Substitute potatoes with 2 cups of grated cauliflower; then squeeze it to remove all water content, and set aside. Season 2 cups wheat flour to taste, then knead cauliflower into it, with 1 tablespoon oil, and a little water, to make a firm dough. Apply some oil, then cover, and refrigerate for 20 minutes.

Spread a dough disc, and add a little oil on it, then make it into a round, flat disc again. Roll and pan fry in the same way as the potato flatbread.

-*Fenugreek Stuffed Flatbread*–*Methi Parantha:* Use ½ cup dry, or 1 cup fresh, washed, and chopped fenugreek leaves. Soak dry leaves *(if using)* in 1 cup water for 10 minutes, until sand settles to the bottom, then spoon it out from the top, and squeeze to remove the water content.

Knead the leaves in 2 cups flour, with salt and red chili powder to taste, plus 1 teaspoon carom seeds crushed between your palms to release its oils. Make a firm dough for easy rolling, then apply a little oil, cover and refrigerate. Follow the remaining steps to roll and pan fry, as in the recipe for cauliflower flatbread..

-*Keema Stuffed Flatbread*–*Keema Parantha:* Substitute potato filling with keema masala, then follow the steps to roll and pan fry, as in the recipe for potato flatbread.

-*Spinach Stuffed Flatbread*–*Palak Parantha:* Substitute fenugreek leaves with 1 cup frozen, or 2 cups fresh chopped spinach. Squeeze the frozen spinach to remove all of the water content. Follow the remaining steps to knead, roll and pan fry, as in the recipe for fenugreek flatbread.

-*Radish Stuffed Flatbread*–*Mooli Parantha:* Substitute cauliflower with grated red radishes, then squeeze to remove all the water content, and set aside. Follow the remaining steps to knead, roll and pan fry, as in the recipe for cauliflower flatbread.

-*Storing Flatbread*–Refrigerate the leftover flatbread in foil, then reheat on the griddle, over medium heat, and serve hot.

-Store them in freezer up to a month. Partially cook them, then let them cool completely. Wrap them in foil, in batches of two, then place in a freezer bag, to prevent having freezer burn.

Defrost them in microwave for a minute, or leave in the fridge a day before, until they can be separated. Heat the griddle and pan fry the flatbread with some oil, until golden-crispy on both sides. Serve hot.

Aloo Parantha *(Potato Stuffed Flatbread) Recipe on P170*

Gobhi Parantha *(Cauliflower Stuffed Flatbread) Recipe on P172*

Methi Parantha *(Fenugreek Stuffed Flatbread) Recipe on P172*

Mooli Parantha *(Radish Stuffed Flatbread) Recipe on P173*

Indian Naan
(Tandoori Flatbread)

Indian Naan is an oval shaped flatbread, with a soft, crispy, and buttery, surface. It is prepared from all-purpose flour and yeast dough, and doesn't take very long to cook. Traditionally, it is cooked in a clay oven, called a *tandoor*, but oven baked naan has the same flavor and taste.

Serves 4 Makes 8
Ingredients:

Prep Time: 15 minutes
Cooking Time: 20 minutes
Inactive Time: 12 hours 45 minutes

2 teaspoons Active Dry Yeast *(Khameer)*
1 teaspoon Sugar *(Chini)*
¾ cup Warm Milk *(Doodh)*
2 cups, plus ½ cup All-Purpose Flour *(Maida)*
1 teaspoon Salt *(Namak)*
5 tablespoons Plain Greek Yogurt *(Dahi)*–divided
2 tablespoons, plus 1 teaspoon Vegetable Oil
¼ cup, plus ¼ cup Water
2 tablespoons Melted Unsalted Butter *(Makkhan)*–for brushing
¼ cup All-Purpose Flour *(Maida)*–for dusting

Method:
For dough; mix together yeast, and sugar in warm milk, then set aside for 10-15 minutes in a warm place, until frothy.

Combine 2 cups flour and salt, in a medium deep bowl, then mix. Make a well in the center, and add 3 tablespoons yogurt; 1 tablespoon oil, and the yeast mixture. Use a wooden spoon to stir all the ingredients, until just combined. The dough should be very loose and sticky.

Brush the dough with little oil, then cover with a plastic wrap, and leave in a warm place, for 12 hours, until it doubles in volume. Add the remaining flour to the dough, then with the wooden spoon, stir again, until it is firmer. Add remaining oil and knead, until elastic and pliable.

Divide the dough into 8 equal portions, then roll and press each into a flat round disc. Cover with a damp paper towel, for another 10 minutes.

Turn on the griddle to medium heat. Dip one disc in dry flour, and roll with a rolling pin, making into an 8 inch oval shape naan. Wet your fingers, using ¼ cup water, and lightly moisten the naan on top, then carefully lift, and place it on the hot griddle, moist side down.

Wait for 1 minute, until it starts to rise on top, and is lightly golden on the underside. Lift it with a flat spoon, and place it on a sheet pan. Repeat the process with the remaining naans, until all are placed on 2 sheet pans *(4 naans on one sheet pan)*. Adjust the heat temperature between medium and low-medium, as needed accordingly.

Whisk the remaining 2 tablespoons yogurt and ¼ cup water to a smooth blend, then brush each naan with that, and place them under the broiler, 4 at a time, for 1-2 minutes, or until they puff up, and are golden on top.

Remove, and lightly brush with melted butter, then serve hot Indian Naan with any meat or vegetarian curry. If eating at a later time; cool and wrap them in foil, and place in a 200 degrees F oven, to keep warm.

Variations:
-*Dough without yeast*: Substitute yeast mixture, with 2 teaspoons baking powder, 1 teaspoon baking soda, ½ cup plain greek yogurt, and ½ cup warm milk, then prepare the dough. Leave the dough in a warm place for 12 hours, until it doubles in volume.

-*Broil without griddle*: Place 4 naans on a greased baking sheet, and place under the broiler for 1-2 minutes until they puff up and become lightly golden.

Flip over, and broil for another minute, until golden. Remove and brush with melted butter, then serve.

-*Cooking over gas burner*: Place the rolled naan on the hot griddle, in the same way as making Tava Roti. Wait for a minute, until lightly cooked on underside. Flip and allow cooking for a minute on the other side.

Remove the naan and place it directly on the gas burner on low-medium flame, for a minute, or until it puffs up and is lightly charred and golden on the underside.

Flip the naan with kitchen tongs, and leave it for 30 seconds, until lightly charred on the other side. Brush with melted butter and serve hot

-Naans can also be prepared in advance. Lightly roast both sides on a warm griddle, then allow them to cool completely. Wrap in plastic wrap, then in foil, and then in freezer bag, and freeze. When needed, just defrost them, then broil as shown in the recipe above, and serve hot .

Indian Naan *(Tandoori Flatbread) Recipe on P175*

Plain Kulcha *(Soft Roasted Flatbread) Recipe on P178*

Plain Kulcha
(Soft Roasted Flatbread)

Plain Kulcha is *soft roasted flatbread*, prepared from all-purpose flour and yeast dough, then griddle roasted. It is part of Punjabi cuisine, and combines well with masala choley, and other curries.

Serves 6, Makes 12
Ingredients:

Prep Time: 15 minutes
Cooking Time: 20 minutes
Inactive Time: 12 hours 15 minutes

1 cup, plus ½ cup Warm Water
1½ teaspoons Sugar *(Chini)*
1 packet Active Dry Yeast *(Khameer)* (2½ teaspoons)
3 cups, plus ½ cup All-Purpose Flour *(Maida)*
1½ teaspoons Salt *(Namak)*
5 tablespoons Plain Greek Yogurt *(Dahi)*
2 tablespoons, plus 1 teaspoon Vegetable Oil
½ cup All-Purpose Flour *(Maida)*–for dusting
¼ cup Melted Unsalted Butter *(Makkhan)*–for brushing

Method:
Combine 1 cup warm water, sugar, and yeast in a bowl, then mix and set aside in a warm place, for 10-15 minutes, or until frothy. In another bowl, combine 3 cups flour and salt, then make a well in the center, and add yogurt, 1 tablespoon oil, and the yeast mixture.

Use a wooden spoon to stir the flour, combining with other ingredients, until just combined. Add the remaining ½ cup water and stir again until well incorporated, about 5 minutes. Brush with little oil, then cover with a plastic wrap, and leave in a warm place, for 12 hours, until it doubles in volume. The dough should be very loose and sticky to touch.

Use the wooden spoon to punch down the dough, releasing all air. Then, add remaining ½ cup flour and stir with the wooden spoon to mix it into the dough, making it little firmer and pliable; for about 5 minutes.

Place the dough on a floured surface, then add remaining 1 tablespoon oil a little at a time, while kneading, until the dough is soft and elastic. Divide it into 12 equal portions. Roll, and press, each between your palms into a round flat disc. Cover them with a moist paper towel.

Heat a cast iron griddle, over medium heat. Dust one disc with dry flour, and roll with a rolling pin, into an 8 inch round. Lift and flip between your hands once, then place it on the hot griddle.

Leave for 30 seconds, until it starts rising, and is lightly golden on the underside. Flip it, with a flat spoon, and leave for 30 seconds, then lightly press on the edges with the flat spoon, until it puffs up, and is lightly roasted, on the other side. Reduce the heat to low-medium, then flip it back, and remove.

Brush the kulcha with melted butter or leave it plain, and serve hot with masala choley, accompanied with onion relish and mint chutney. Repeat, to roll and cook the remaining kulchas, until all are done.

For a later serving time, cool and wrap kulchas in foil, and leave in a 200 degrees F oven, to keep warm, until the serving time.

Variations:
-*Potato-Peas Soft Flatbread*–*Aloo Matar Kulcha:* Stuff 1 tablespoon of potato-peas filling, in each dough disc; then seal it securely *(same stuffing as in the potato stuffed flatbread with added ¼ cup of cooked peas–P170)*. Cover and set aside for 2 minutes. Lightly roll to an 8 by 8 inch round, then roast in the same way as plain kulcha. Brush with butter and serve hot.

-*Onion Soft Flatbread*–*Pyaz Kulcha:* Substitute potato-peas mix with 1 minced onion, plus 2 tablespoons chopped cilantro, seasoned with salt and red chili powder to taste. Then, follow the remaining steps as in the recipe for potato-peas kulcha.

-*Cheese Soft Flatbread*–*Paneer Kulcha:* Substitute potato-peas mix with 1 cup seasoned and mashed homemade cottage cheese. Then, follow the remaining steps as in the recipe for potato-peas kulcha.

-*Keema Masala Soft Flatbread*–*Keema Kulcha:* Substitute potato-peas mix with 1 cup keema masala for the stuffing. Then, follow the remaining steps as in the recipe for potato-peas kulcha.

-*Spinach Fenugreek Soft Flatbread*–*Palak Methi Kulcha:* Substitute potato-pea's mix with 1 cup fresh chopped spinach and fenugreek leaves' mix. Squeeze to remove all their water content; then stuff in the dough disc with seasoning to taste. Then, follow the remaining steps as in the recipe for potato-peas kulcha.

Indian Sweets and Baked Treats

Indian Sweets are called *'mithai'* in India. As an old tradition, they are eaten after every meal. Since these days everyone is health conscious, I have tried to make them as low fat as possible, using low fat milk, more oil, and less ghee–*clarified butter.*

Some of the popular sweets are: Carrot Pudding–*Gajar Halwa,* Sweet Cottage Cheese Dumplings–*Rasgoola,* Coconut Fudge–*Nariyal Burfi,* Dark Sweet Milk Dumplings–*Kaala Jaam,* Gram Flour Fudge–*Besan Burfi,* Gram Flour Sweet Balls–*Besan Laddoo,* Gram Flour Sweet Puff Balls–*Boondi Laddoo,* Milk Fudge–*Khoya Burfi,* Mini Funnel Cake–*Jalebi,* Pistachio Ice Cream–*Pista Kulfi,* Rice Pudding–*Chawal Kheer,* Vermicelli Pudding–*Sevian Kheer,* Sweet Milk Dumplings–*Gulab Jamun,* and many more.

When I was in Africa, I taught myself to make all Indian sweets, as they were not available in stores. I still prefer to make sweets at home, as much as possible, so I can control the amount of sugar, and butter, or clarified butter, that I use in making them. Homemade sweets are always better than store bought.

Besan Burfi *(Gram Flour Fudge)*

Besan Burfi
(Gram Flour Fudge)

Besan Burfi is *gram flour fudge*, prepared from gram flour, sugar, and clarified butter. It is sweet and delicious, like candy.

Serves 12, Makes 24 Squares
Ingredients:
1½ cups Gram Flour *(Besan)*
1 cup Sugar *(Chini)*
2/3 cup Clarified Butter *(Ghee)* or Melted Unsalted Butter *(Makkhan)*
½ teaspoon Green Cardamom Powder *(Pisi Choti Ilaichi)*
1/3 cup Slivered Almonds, Pistachio, Cashews *(Badam, Pista, Kaju)*
Also Needed: A Heavy Base Wok or Karahi

Prep Time: 10 minutes
Cooking Time: 35 minutes
Inactive Time: 2 hours 25 minutes

Method:
Combine gram flour, and clarified butter in a wok, then mix well. Turn on the heat to medium, then cook and stir constantly, to prevent burning, for about 20-25 minutes, until the flour mix smells roasted-sweet, and clarified butter separates. Turn off the heat.

Mix in the cardamom and 1 teaspoon of nuts to the roasted fudge mix. Then, set aside for 15 minutes, until the fudge mix cools down to a warm temperature. Add sugar, and mix, until it is distributed evenly.

Transfer the fudge mix, into an 10 by 10 inch pre-greased *(using little ghee)* square pan. Tap the pan to spread the mix evenly. Sprinkle the remaining nuts as garnish on top, and press gently, to stick them.

Set aside for 2 hours, or refrigerate, if temperature is too warm, until the fudge is completely cool and set. Remove, and leave out for 10 minutes, then cut into 1 inch squares, and store in an airtight container. Besan Burfi can stay outside for a week, in winters, then refrigerate for a longer time. In summers, refrigerate after cutting it.

Variations:
-*Gram Flour Sweet Balls*–*Besan Laddoo*: Take a medium scoop of fudge mix in your hand, then press gently but firmly to bind the laddoos together, until a round ball forms. Stick and press a piece of pistachio, as a garnish. Repeat, to make the remaining laddoos, then store them in an airtight container.

Nariyal Burfi
(Coconut Fudge)

Nariyal Burfi is a traditional South Indian *coconut fudge,* prepared from milk powder, desiccated coconut, and clarified butter. This is a soft, and creamy fudge; it just melts in your mouth. Nariyal Burfi has been the favorite Indian sweet in my family.

Serves 12, Makes 24 Squares
Ingredients:

Prep Time: 10 minutes
Cooking Time: 50 minutes
Inactive Time: 2 hours 10 minutes

1 cup Milk Powder–from Indian Store
1/3 cup, plus ½ teaspoon Clarified Butter *(Ghee)*
2/3 cup 2% Milk *(Doodh)*
½ cup Sugar *(Chini)*
1 drop Red Food Color
1 cup Fine Unsweetened Desiccated Coconut *(Nariyal)*
¼ cup Slivered Almonds, Pistachio, Cashews *(Badam, Pista, Kaju)*
2 drops Kewra Essence–from Indian Store
OR ¼ teaspoon Green Cardamom Powder *(Pisi Choti Ilaichi)*

Method:
Combine milk powder, clarified butter, and milk, in a non-stick wok or karahi, then whisk, for about 5 minutes, until smooth.

Turn on the heat to low-medium. Then, cook and stir constantly, to prevent burning, for about 10-15 minutes, until the mixture changes color to a pale yellow, and smells roasted-sweet; it leaves the edges of the wok, and the clarified butter separates.

Remove from heat and add sugar, then mix, until completely dissolved. Add the red food color, then mix again, to bring an even light pink color. Then, add coconut, and mix, until incorporated well.

Bring it back to low-medium heat; then cook for 10-15 minutes, stirring constantly, to prevent burning, until coconut smells roasted.

Turn off the heat, and add 1 tablespoon of mixed nuts, and cardamom or kewra essence - whichever you have on hand. Then, mix to distribute the nuts evenly; and allow cooling for 5 minutes. Transfer the fudge mix into a 10 by 10 inch pre-greased *(using little ghee)* square or round pan, then tap it to spread the mix evenly.

Sprinkle a few drops of kewra essence on the fudge, then spread evenly with a spatula. Spread the remaining nuts on top in a single layer, and press gently to stick them. Set aside to cool completely, or refrigerate if the temperature is warm, for about 2 hours.

Remove and leave the fudge out for 5 minutes, then loosen it from the edges with a butter knife. Dip the knife in water, then cut into 1 inch squares. Store in a plastic container, and refrigerate for a month.

Variations:
-For *Plain Milk Fudge*–Plain Khoya Burfi, exclude the coconut and red food color, then follow the steps as in recipe above.

Nariyal Burfi *(Coconut Fudge)*

Plain Khoya Burfi *(Plain Milk Fudge)*

Gajar Halwa
(Carrot Pudding)

Gajar Halwa–*carrot pudding*, is a traditional Punjabi dessert, and is also known as *gajrela*. It is prepared from fresh grated carrots, clarified butter, milk, and dry fruits. For this recipe, I have used 2% milk to keep it light, without compromising the taste.

Serves 6
Ingredients:
Prep Time: 15 minutes
Cooking Time: 1 hour 35 minutes

4 tablespoons Clarified Butter *(Ghee)*–divided
4 cups Grated Carrots *(Gajar)*–about 8 medium carrots
2½ cups 2% Milk *(Doodh)*
½ cup Sugar *(Chini)*
1 teaspoon Green Cardamom Powder *(Pisi Choti Ilaichi)*
3 tablespoons Chopped Cashew, Pistachio, Almonds *(Kaju, Pista, Badam)*
pinch of Saffron *(Zafran)*
For Khoya: (Thickened Milk)
2 tablespoons 2% Milk *(Doodh)*
1/3 cup Milk Powder–from Indian Store
1 tablespoon Clarified Butter *(Ghee)*

Method:

Heat 2 tablespoons of clarified butter in a non-stick wok or a heavy base skillet, over low-medium heat. Add carrots and sauté them for 5 minutes, until light pale in color.

Add milk, and mix well. Increase the heat to medium, and stir the milk constantly, until it comes to a boil, for about 8 minutes.

Reduce the heat to low-medium. Cover, and cook for 30 minutes, until carrots are tender. Stir every 5 minutes, to prevent burning.

Reduce the heat further to low, then partially cover, and cook for another 15 minutes, until most of the milk has evaporated. Stir a few times in between to prevent burning.

Add 1 more tablespoon of clarified butter; the sugar, cardamom, and 2 tablespoons mixed nuts, then gently mix. Uncover and cook for 20 minutes, gently stirring every 5 minutes. Turn off the heat, and set aside.

To make *khoya*, combine milk powder, milk, and clarified butter, in a non-stick pan, then mix well. Cook for 5 minutes, over low heat, stirring constantly, until it smells roasted, and not raw. Turn off the heat.

Add the remaining 1 tablespoon of clarified butter, and khoya, to the carrot mix, then gently fold in everything, until incorporated well.

Simmer, for another 10 minutes, uncovered, then give it a final gentle mix, and turn off the heat. Transfer Gajar Halwa into a serving dish, then garnish with remaining mixed nuts, and saffron. Serve hot.

To serve later, let it cool completely, then cover and refrigerate without the garnish. Microwave for 2 minutes, then garnish and serve.

Note: Be patient when making Gajar Halwa, for best results. The more you cook it over low heat, the better it tastes.

Variations:
-*Carrot Milk Pudding*–*Gajar Kheer:* Add 2 more cups milk, plus sugar to the carrots. Cook for 10 minutes, stirring constantly, over medium heat, until the milk comes to a boil. Reduce the heat to low-medium, then partially cover and cook for 30 minutes, or until it starts to thicken. Reduce the heat to low, then cook for 30 minutes, until it is thick like rice pudding. Stir every 5 minutes, to prevent burning. Adjust sugar to taste.

Gajar Halwa *(Carrot Halwa)*

Chawal Kheer
(Rice Pudding)

Chawal Kheer–*rice pudding,* is a rich dessert, prepared from rice, milk, sugar, and flavorings like: cardamom, kewra essence, and saffron; and nuts like: almonds, pistachio and cashews. It is cooked during festivals; as offering (*prasadam*) for prayers; or on special occasions.

Serves 6
Ingredients:

Prep Time: 15 minutes
Cooking Time: 1 hour 25 minutes
Inactive Time: 2 hours 15 minutes

¼ cup Basmati Rice (*Basmati Chawal*)
1 cup Water–for soaking rice
4 cups Whole Milk (*Doodh*)
¼ cup Sugar (*Chini*)–add more as needed
½ teaspoon Green Cardamom Powder (*Pisi Choti Ilaichi*)
1 tablespoon Unsalted Butter (*Makkhan*)
¼ cup Chopped Almonds, Pistachio, Cashews (*Badam, Pista, Kaju*)
pinch of Saffron (*Zafran*)
2 drops Kewra Essence (*optional*)

Method:
Gently rinse the rice 3-4 times in water, or until the water is clear, then soak in 1 cup water, for 15 minutes.

Meanwhile, combine milk, sugar, and cardamom, in a heavy base pot. Then, turn on the heat to medium, and stir constantly, until the sugar dissolves, and the milk starts to boil, for about 10-12 minutes. Turn off the heat, and set aside, to use later.

Melt the butter in a heavy base wok, over low-medium heat, then strain the rice, and add to it. Stir-fry, for 2 minutes, until lightly golden. Remove the wok from heat, and add milk, then mix. Bring it back to heat, and increase it to medium. Stir constantly, until the milk comes to a boil.

Reduce the heat to low-medium; partially cover, and cook for 30 minutes, stirring often. Add half each, the nuts and saffron; then gently stir. Further, reduce the heat to low, and continue cooking, still partially covered; for 30 more minutes, until the milk reduces by one third (1.3 cups), and the pudding thickens enough, to coat the back of a spoon.

Stir every 5 minutes, scraping the cream from the sides of the wok, and mixing it back in to the milk. This is the key to making the pudding thick, rich, and creamy.

Turn off the heat and let it cool, then add kewra essence, and gently stir, to distribute it evenly.

Transfer into a serving dish; cover and refrigerate for 2 hours before serving. Garnish with remaining nuts and saffron, then serve.

Chawal Kheer can be served hot or cold, and can be made a day in advance and refrigerated without garnish. Then, serve with the garnish.

Variation:
-*Indian Vermicelli Pudding*–*Sevian Kheer:* Substitute rice with sevian–*Indian vermicelli,* plus 2 cups milk; then follow the recipe for rice pudding. It cooks in about 30 minutes, and is much softer than rice pudding so keep the heat low, while cooking. Add sugar to taste.

-*The Foxnut Pudding*–*Makhane Ki Kheer:* Substitute rice with makhane–*Foxnuts,* plus 2 cups milk. It cooks in about 30 minutes; is creamier, and richer. Keep the heat low while cooking, and add sugar to taste.

Tip: Add 1 teaspoon extra sugar if serving chilled *(optional).*

Chawal Kheer *(Rice Pudding)*

Rasgoola
(Sugar Syrup Dumplings)

Rasgoola is a soft, spongy, and sweet dessert from the state of Orissa in India. It is prepared from fresh cottage cheese dumplings, cooked in sugar syrup–*chashni*. As a child, my father used to trick me into taking bitter medicines whenever I was sick, by offering me rasgoola, and I would always agree to take them. What a treat!

Serves 12, Makes 32 Small Dumplings
Ingredients:
2 cups Fresh Cottage Cheese *(Paneer)*
Refer to Recipe on P111
For Sugar Syrup: *(Chashni)*
3 cups Sugar *(Chini)*
9 cups Hot Tap Water (reduces cooking time)
For Garnish:
¼ teaspoon Kewra Essence or pinch of Saffron *(Zafran)*
¼ cup Chopped Almonds, Pistachio, Cashew *(Badam, Pista, Kaju)*

Prep Time: 25 minutes
Cooking Time: 35 minutes
Inactive Time: 2 hours

Method:
To make *rasgoola*; squeeze and remove the water from cottage cheese as much as possible; then place it on to a clean work surface. Knead the cheese with the heels of your hand, for about 10-15 minutes, until a soft dough forms. The more you knead, the softer it gets.

Use a big melon scoop to divide the cheese dough into 32 equal portions, then roll each between your palms, into a smooth round ball. Set them aside on a plate, and cover with a damp paper towel, to prevent drying.

For *simple sugar syrup*; combine sugar, and water in a wide deep pot, then stir. Turn on the heat to high, and continue to stir, until the syrup comes to a boil, and the sugar dissolves completely; about 8 minutes.

Add the first batch of 16 cheese balls into the boiling sugar syrup, then cover tightly with the lid. Allow them to steam in the syrup, for 7 minutes over high heat, until they puff up, and are double in size. Reduce the heat to medium, and steam for 5 more minutes, until they cook through.

Turn down the heat to low, and transfer the first batch of dumplings into a bowl, along with some of the syrup, then cover them and set aside. Dumplings should be spongy, when squeezed.

Turn up the heat back to high, and repeat the process for the second batch of dumplings. When all the dumplings are ready, sprinkle saffron on top, then cover, and set aside, to cool completely.

Saffron gives a light yellow color and has a unique flavor and aroma; this brings a sophisticated look to the whole dish.

Transfer the rasgoolas into a serving bowl, and refrigerate for 2 hours before serving. Garnish with kewra essence, pistachios, almonds and cashews to give that royal look, then serve chilled.

Tip: After Rasgoolas are finished, save the leftover syrup and cook it further to convert into a 1 string consistency sugar syrup *(P193)*. Cool and refrigerate in a clean jar. Use in making pista kulfi.

Variations:
-*Sweet Milk Syrup Dumplings*–*Ras Malai*: Make the cheese dumplings into round flat discs, then follow the recipe to make sugar syrup dumplings. When they are done, set them aside, to cool completely.

Boil the milk, with sugar, as in the recipe for rice pudding, without the cardamom, until it is reduced by one third, and has thickend. Turn off the heat, and set aside to cool.

Squeeze the dumplings from the sugar syrup, and add to the creamy milk syrup; which they will soak up and become creamier. Add kewra essence, and cardamom, then garnish with dry nuts, and serve chilled.

-*Cottage Cheese Pudding*–*Paneer Ki Kheer*: Cut the cottage cheese into small cubes, and cook them in milk with sugar, and cardamom powder over low-medium heat, stirring often, until milk is reduced by one third, and has thickened. Garnish with mixed chopped nuts and serve chilled.

-*Stuffed Sweet Rasgoola*–*Rajbhog*: Stuff cheese balls with khoya *(P185)*, mixed with nuts; then follow the steps as in recipe for rasgoola.

Rasgoola *(Sugar Syrup Dumplings) Recipe on P188*

Pista Kulfi *(Pistachio Ice Cream)*

Pista Kulfi
(Pistachio Ice Cream)

Pista Kulfi is creamy, nutty, rich, and flavorful *pistachio ice cream*, prepared from whole milk, nuts, and flavorings. It is a favorite summer time dessert, and is a sophisticated sweet item on special occasions.

Serves 12, Makes 12　　　　　　　*Prep Time: 15 minutes*
Ingredients:　　　　　　　　　　*Cooking Time: 1 hour 30 minutes*
4 cups Whole Milk *(Doodh)*　　　　*Inactive Time: 6 hours 30 minutes*
½ teaspoon Green Cardamom Powder *(Pisi Choti Ilaichi)*
2 teaspoons Sugar Syrup–*Chashni (P193)* or 2 teaspoons Glucose Syrup
2 tablespoons Ground Pistachio *(Pisa Pista)*
pinch of Saffron *(Zafran)*
1 tablespoon Slivered Pistachio *(Pista)*
1 teaspoon Slivered Almonds *(Badam)*
1 teaspoon Slivered Cashews *(Kaju)*
A few drops of Kewra Essence
Also Needed: 12 Kulfi Molds or 6 small Glass Ramekins

Method:

Combine milk, cardamom, and sugar syrup in a wide heavy base pot, then mix. Turn on the heat to high, and stir constantly to prevent burning, until the milk comes to a boil, about 12 minutes.

Reduce the heat to low-medium, then partially cover, and cook for 60 minutes, or until the milk is reduced by half (2 cups). Stir every 10 minutes; scraping the cream from the sides of the pot, and mixing it back in the milk, which makes it thick, and creamy.

Add ground pistachio, and half the saffron, then stir, until mixed well. Turn off the heat. Set aside to cool completely, for 30 minutes, then add kewra essence and mix.

Whisk the kulfi mixture by hand or with a hand mixer for 2-5 minutes, or until it is smooth without any lumps of cream. Whisking prevents the forming of any ice crystals when kulfi is frozen.

Cover and refrigerate the mixture for 2 hours before freezing it. Whisk one more time, then pour the mixture in the molds, to about 2/3 full, or in the ramekins, to about 3/4 full. Cover with lids, or foil, and freeze for 4 hours.

For Serving, remove the kulfi molds from the freezer, and leave out for 2 minutes to defrost. Loosen the kulfi from the molds with a butter knife, then place on a serving plate. Garnish with mixed nuts and remaining saffron, and serve. Ramekins can be garnished and served individually.

Variations:
-Substitute 50% milk with condensed milk, which is sweeter; then follow the recipe for kulfi as above without the sugar syrup.
-Substitute 50% milk with heavy cream, and follow the recipe, keeping the remaining ingredients as same.

-*Mango Kulfi*: Substitute 50% milk with heavy cream, then add sugar syrup. Follow the recipe for pista kulfi, for cooking without the cardamom and nuts. Remove and allow cooling. Add 2 cups mango pulp, and mix. Blend in a food processor, until smooth. Mix in some saffron, then follow the instructions to freeze and serve mango kulfi as indicated above.

-*Plain Kulfi*: Boil, then simmer the mixture of milk, cream, sugar syrup, and cardamom, until it is reduced by half. Turn off the heat, then follow the remaining steps as in the recipe for pista kulfi without the nuts.

Jalebi *(Indian Funnel Cake)*

Jalebi
(Indian Funnel Cake)

Jalebi is like *funnel cake*; it is crispy on the outside and soft and full of sweet syrup on the inside. This is a quick and easy recipe, prepared from all-purpose flour and yeast batter. I used to make Jalebi all the time when I was in Africa, and my friends would stand in the kitchen and eat them fresh and hot from the stove, as I was making them.

Serves 12, Makes 36 Small Jalebi
Ingredients:
For Batter:
1 cup All-Purpose Flour *(Maida)*
1 teaspoon Active Dry Yeast *(Khameer)*
½ teaspoon Sugar *(Chini)*
1 teaspoon Corn Starch
½ cup Plain Greek Yogurt *(Dahi)*
1 teaspoon Vegetable Oil
½ cup Warm Water
4 drops Yellow Food Color

For Sugar Syrup:
2 cups Sugar *(Chini)*
1 cup Water
2 tablespoons Lemon Juice *(Neembu Rus)*

Also Needed:
1 empty Plastic Sauce Bottle
1 cup Canola Oil–to fry

Prep Time: 20 minutes
Cooking Time: 40 minutes
Inactive Time: 1 hour 10 minutes

Method:
Combine flour, yeast, sugar, corn starch, yogurt, and oil, in a bowl, then whisk until smooth. Slowly add water, while mixing, until well combined. Whip for 10 minutes, until smooth batter forms. Cover and leave in a warm place, for 1 hour to ferment.

Meanwhile, prepare 1 string consistency *sugar syrup*–*chashni*. Heat the sugar and water in a wide pan, over low-medium heat, until sugar dissolves completely, and the syrup is thick and bubbly, about 10 minutes. Allow it to cool a little, then take a drop of syrup and press between your index finger and thumb, then pull apart. If it forms a single string thread, the syrup is ready to use. Add lemon juice to it and mix. It prevents forming sugar crystals after jalebi is hard.

Heat the oil in a non-stick skillet over low-medium heat. Add the food color to the batter and mix, to get an even saffron color.

Pour the batter in the sauce bottle until it is half full; then close the lid tight. Test the oil by squeezing a drop of batter in it. It should sizzle and rise to the top in 30 seconds and not turn brown. The oil is ready to use.

Carefully squeeze the batter in the hot oil in a circular motion, making 2 circles, one inside the other, then make a line across to join them; to make into the shape of a mini funnel cake.

Continue making 3 more mini funnel cakes, and stop. Fry in batches of four, for 30 seconds on each side, until lightly golden and crispy.

With a slotted spoon, slide each funnel cake to the side of the pan, to drain excess oil; then transfer into the sugar syrup. Make sure the syrup is hot enough to seep through the tiny holes in the funnel cake quickly.

Soak for 10 seconds on each side, until the funnel cakes are filled with syrup. Bring to the side to drain excess syrup, then transfer them onto a plate, until they cool down, and harden on the outside, about 1 minute.

Repeat the process until all the batter is finished. Serve Jalebi hot or at room temperature. It is sweet, tangy and crispy on the outside; and soft, syrupy on the inside.

Enjoy after meals or anytime, and store in a container. Jalebi can stay at room temperature during winter, but needs refrigeration in summers.

Variations:
-Substitute the white flour with gram flour to prepare the batter; then follow the recipe as above to prepare the jalebi.

-Make the batter without the yogurt; then follow the recipe as above to prepare the jalebi.

-Make the batter without yeast, then whip to make it smooth. Leave the batter in a warm place for 12 hours to ferment. Whip again; then follow the remaining steps as in recipe above to prepare the jalebi.

Banana Pecan Bread

Banana Pecan Bread is moist, nutty, flavorful; and very easy to make. The traditional recipe requires eggs, but this recipe doesn't, and it tastes delicious. This is very good as an evening snack with tea.

Serves: 6
Ingredients:

Prep Time: 25 minutes
Cooking Time: 1 hour 10 minutes
Inactive Time: 30 minutes

5 Full Ripe Bananas
1 ½ cups All-Purpose Flour *(Maida)*
1 teaspoon Baking Powder
1 teaspoon Baking Soda
¼ teaspoon Salt *(Namak)*
¾ cup Melted Unsalted Butter *(Makkhan)*
¾ cup Sugar *(Chini)*
¾ cup Chopped Pecans *(Chota Akhrot)*
2 tablespoons Chopped Almonds and Pistachio *(Badam, Pista)*
2 tablespoons Golden Raisins *(Kishmish)*

Also Needed:
4 by 8 inch size Loaf Pan
1 teaspoon Butter, plus 1 tablespoon Flour–for greasing

Method:
Peel and mash all the bananas in a bowl with a fork, to make a smooth puree, then cover and set aside.

Combine flour, baking powder, baking soda and salt in another bowl and mix well. Add butter and sugar to the flour mixture, and mix again, to evenly distribute the ingredients.

Add banana puree, pecans, almonds, pistachio, and raisins, then mix again, to incorporate everything well. Grease and flour the loaf pan, then pour the banana batter in it, and bake in a preheated oven at 350 degrees F, for 1 hour.

Turn off the oven, and leave the banana bread, for another 10 minutes, to complete the rest of the baking. Insert a toothpick; and if it comes out clean, the banana bread is ready, otherwise leave it in for a few more minutes, until it is fully baked.

Remove, and let it cool for 15 minutes, then loosen the bread from the edges of the pan with a butter knife, and place it on a cooling rack for another 15 minutes. Cut the bread into 8 slices and serve with tea.

Banana Pecan Bread, *Recipe on P195*

Fruit Cookies

Fruit Cookies

Fruit Cookies are colorful and delicious; crunchy on the outside and moist on the inside. These are prepared from candied fruits.

Serves 15, Makes 30 Cookies
Ingredients:

Prep Time: 1 hour
Cooking Time: 20 minutes
Inactive Time: 18 hours

¾ cup Chopped Pitted Dates *(Khajoor)*
½ cup Golden Raisins *(Kishmish)*
3 tablespoons Chopped Candied Cherries
2 tablespoons Chopped Dried Apricots *(Khumani)*
½ cup Chopped Candied Pineapples *(Anannās)*
¾ cup Chopped Pecans *(Chota Akhrot)*
1½ teaspoons Honey *(Shehad)*
½ tablespoon Freshly Squeezed Lemon Juice *(Neembu Rus)*
1 tablespoon Balsamic Vinegar *(Sirka)*
½ teaspoon Salt *(Namak)*–divided
1 stick Unsalted Butter *(Makkhan)*–at room temperature
½ cup Sugar *(Chini)*
½ teaspoon Ground Cloves *(Pisi Laung)*
1 large Egg
2 cups All-Purpose Flour *(Maida)*
1 teaspoon Baking Soda
1 teaspoon Baking Powder

Method:

In a medium bowl, combine the dates, raisins, cherries, apricots, pineapples, pecans, honey, lemon juice, vinegar, and ¼ teaspoon salt, then mix well. Cover and refrigerate overnight. The salt will help rehydrate the fruits, and release their juices.

In another bowl, or an electric mixer; cream butter, sugar, and cloves, until light, fluffy, and smooth, about 6 minutes. Mix in the egg, until well incorporated. Add flour, baking soda, baking powder, and remaining salt to the butter mixture, then mix, until just combined. Don't over mix. Add and fold in the fruits, along with the liquid, to the flour mix, until evenly distributed.

Divide the dough into 2 halves, and place each half on separate 15 by 18 inch piece of parchment paper. Roll each into a log, 1½ to 2 inches thick, and 10 inches long. Refrigerate for 5 hours, until firm, and easy to slice.

Remove the parchment paper, and slice the dough logs with a paring knife, into ½ inch thick rounds. Place them ½ inch apart, on 2 baking sheets, lined with parchment paper. Then, bake in a preheated oven at 350 degrees F, for 20 minutes, until lightly golden.

Remove, and let them cool for 10 minutes, then transfer on to a cooling rack to completely cool. These are sweet, tart, and chewy on the inside, and crunchy on the outside. Serve with evening tea.

Chocolate Granola Squares

I always wanted to make granola squares at home because they are good for health, and I can control the ingredients that I put in them. I have been experimenting with different recipes, until I got this one successfully. Feel free to change the ingredients to your liking.

Serves 24, Makes 24 Squares
Ingredients:

Prep Time: 25 minutes
Cooking Time: 40 minutes
Inactive Time: 4 hours

4 tablespoons Unsalted Butter *(Makkhan)*
2 cups Old-Fashioned Quaker Oats
1 cup Chopped, Cashews, Almonds, Peanuts *(Kaju, Badam, Mungphali)*
½ cup Unsweetened Shredded Coconut *(Nariyal)*
½ cup Honey *(Shehad)*
½ cup Brown Sugar *(Chini)*
2 teaspoons Vanilla Essence
1/3 cup Unsweetened Cocoa Powder
½ teaspoon Salt *(Namak)*
3 cups Chopped Dried Apricots, Pitted Dates, Raisins *(Khumani, Khajoor, Kishmish)*
½ cup Roasted Wheat Germ

Method:
Prepare a 10 by 10 inch square pan by greasing with ½ teaspoon butter, then set aside to use later for setting the granola.

Heat a non-stick pan over low-medium heat, then dry roast the oats and the mixed nuts together, for 4-5 minutes; then the coconut for 2 minutes; until they all smell roasted; being sure not to burn them. Alltogether, it takes 6-7 minutes to roast them. Set aside to cool, and use later.

Combine honey, brown sugar, remaining butter, vanilla, cocoa powder, and salt, in a small saucepan, then turn on the heat to low-medium

Stir, until the butter melts; the cocoa and sugar dissolves. Simmer for 3 minutes, until a thin sugar syrup forms. It smells and tastes delicious.

Note: Adjust honey, brown sugar and butter according to your taste.

Mix in the dried fruits, and wheat germ, to the roasted oats mixture; then pour the hot sugar syrup on top. Use a wooden spoon to stir everything really well, until it is completely coated in sugar syrup.

Transfer the hot granola, into the prepared pan. Press it down with a moist wooden spoon, until smooth into an even compact layer. Place a piece of parchment or wax paper, and press down the granola; then place another 10 by 10 inch square empty pan on top. Now to press and compact further, place a kettle full of water on top.

Set aside the granola to cool completely, for about 3-4 hours. If the temperature is too warm, refrigerate it for 4 hours, and replace the kettle with 2 yogurt containers. Leave the granola out for 5 minutes, then remove it from the pan, on to a cutting board. Cut into 2 inch squares, and you make 24 pieces in total.

Wrap each granola square in plastic wrap, then store in a container. Refrigerate in the summer, and leave them out in winter. Enjoy them for breakfast, or a midday or evening snack. They are a healthy and chewy treat at any time of the day.

Chocolate Granola Squares

Menu Ideas

Breakfast, Lunch, Evening Snack, and Dinner Menu Ideas:

Breakfast Indian Style:

Vegetarian:
- Aloo Parantha - *Potato Stuffed Flatbread* – P170
- Gobhi Parantha - *Cauliflower Stuffed Flatbread* – P172
- Methi Parantha - *Fenugreek Stuffed Flatbread* – P172
- Mooli Parantha - *Radish Stuffed Flatbread* – P173
- Palak Parantha - *Spinach Stuffed Flatbread* – P173
- Meetha Dalia - *Sweet Cream of Wheat* – P123
- Neembu Cheeley - *Lemon Crepes* – P126
- Sooji Upma - *Semolina Polenta* – P121

Non-Vegetarian:
- Keema Parantha - *Keema Stuffed Flatbread* – P173
- Murg or Machchi Pakora - *Chicken or Fish Fritters* – P116

  Accompaniments:
  - Imli Ki Chutney - *Tamarind Chutney* – P27
  - Podiney Ki Chutney - *Mint Chutney* – P24
  - Aam Ki Chutney - *Mango Chutney* – P29
  - Aam Ki Lassi - *Mango Smoothie* – P15
  - Kheera Raita - *Cucumber Yogurt Sauce* – P57
  - Mooli Lachcha - *Radish Relish* – P30
  - Neembu Pani - *Fresh Lemonade* – P17
  - Pyaz Ka Lachcha - *Onion Relish* – P31
  - Timatar Ki Chutney – *Tomato Chutney* – P26

Lunch Indian Style:

Vegetarian:
- Aloo Tikki Sandwich - *Potato Cutlet Sandwich* – P42
- Baingan Palak Pizza - *Eggplant Spinach Pizza* – P44
- Baingan Sandwich - *Eggplant Sandwich* – P39
- Gobhi Makai Soup - *Cauliflower Corn Soup* – P37
- Hash Sandwich - *Sweet Potato Corn Hash Sandwich* – P137
- Khumbi Lobhiya Soup - *Mushroom Black-Eyed Pea Soup* – P35
- Pizza Sandwich – P40
- Subzi Pizza - *Vegetable Garden Pizza* – P43
- Shimla Mirch Makai Soup - *Bell Pepper Corn Soup* – P34
- Timatar Sandwich - *Open Tomato Sandwich* – P40
- Tori Sandwich - *Zucchini Sandwich* – P40

Lunch Indian Style Contd.

Vegetarian:

- Alfredo Florentine - *Spinach Pasta in White Sauce* – P46
- Baingan Lasagna - *Eggplant Lasagna* – P48
- Baingan Parmesan - *Eggplant Parmesan* – P87
- Bhurma Baingan - *Stuffed Baby Eggplant* – P89
- Dal Palak - *Lentil Spinach Soup* – P69
- Dal Tadka - *Tempered Lentil Soup* – P67
- Kadhi Pakori - *Gram Flour Dumplings Curry* – P91
- Rajma Curry - *Red Kidney Beans Curry* – P73
- Rasa Pakori - *Lentil Dumplings Curry* – P107
- Sukhi Urad - *Tempered Dry Urad Lentils* – P71
- Aloo Khumbi Pulao - *Potato Mushroom Pilaf* - P59
- Kichadi - *Lentil Rice Polenta* – P64

Non-Vegetarian:

- Bhuni Machchi Sandwich - *Grilled Fish Sandwich* – P148
- Cornish Pasty - *Meat Pie* – P161
- Machchi Taco - *Fish Taco* – P149
- Murg Pie - *Chicken Pie* – P159
- Murg Tikka Masala - *Spicy Chicken Tikka* – P141
- Sausage Roll – *Meat Roll* – P163
- Tandoori Machchi - *Broiled Fish* – P147

Accompaniments:

- Aam Ki Lassi - *Mango Smoothie* – P15
- Aloo Ka Bhurta - *Mashed Potatoes* – P50
- Bhuna Papadam - *Roasted Lentil Cracker* – P32
- Gajar Ki Kanji - *Carrot Beverage* – P22
- Ghiya Raita - *Bottle Gourd Yogurt Sauce* – P58
- Kheera Raita - *Cucumber Yogurt Sauce* – P57
- Podiney Raita - *Mint Yogurt Sauce* – P57
- Subzi Raita - *Vegetable Yogurt Sauce* – P57
- Aam Ki Chutney - *Mango Chutney* - P29
- Mooli Lachcha - *Radish Relish* – P30
- Plain Parantha - *Plain Pan Fried Flatbread* – P172
- Pyaz Ka Lachcha - *Onion Relish* – P31
- Tava Roti - *Griddle Roasted Wheat Flatbread* – P166
- Timatar Ki Chutney - *Tomato Chutney* – P26
- Zafrani Chawal - *Saffron Rice* – P61
- Pico-De-Gallo - *Salsa* – P149

Snacks Indian Style:
Vegetarian:
- Aloo Tikki - *Potato Cutlet – P113*
- Baingan Cutlet - *Eggplant Cutlet – P39*
- Bandgobhi Bonda - *Cabbage Dumplings – P124*
- Dahi Saunth Pakori - *Yogurt Tamarind Dumplings – P52*
- Dahi Vada - *Yogurt Lentil Doughnuts – P55*
- Kofta Pakori - *Vegetable Dumplings – P96.*
- Kurkuree Hari Phali - *Crispy Green Beans – P117*
- Moong Dal Pakori - *Moong Lentil Dumplings – P52*
- Subzi Pakora - *Vegetable Fritter – P115*
- Subzi Roll - *Vegetable Roll – P134*
- Sooji Dhokla - *Savory Semolina Cake – P119*
- Urad Dal Vada - *Urad Lentil Doughnuts – P55*
- Vegetable Samosa - *Vegetable Stuffed Pastry – P128*
- Baked Namak Pare - *Baked Savory Squares – P132*
- Banana Pistachio Bread *– P195*
- Besan Burfi - *Gram Flour Fudge – P181*
- Fruit Cookies *– P197*
- Chocolate Granola Squares *– P198*
- Nariyal Burfi - *Coconut Fudge – P182*
- Plain Khoya Burfi - *Plain Milk Fudge - P183*

Non-Vegetarian:
- Keema Samosa - *Meat Samosa – 130*
- Machchi Pakora - *Fish Fritter – P116*
- Meat Kofta - *Meat Ball – P155*
- Murg Pakora - *Chicken Fritter – P116*

Accompaniments:
- Aam Ki Lassi - *Mango Smoothie – P15*
- Gajar Ki Kanji - *Carrot Beverage – P22*
- Imli Ki Chutney - *Tamarind Chutney –P27*
- Jal Zeera Pani - *Cumin Water – P20*
- Neembu Pani- *Fresh Lemonade – P17*
- Podiney Ki Chutney - *Mint Chutney – P24*
- Podiney Ki Lassi - *Savory Mint Smoothie – P17*

Dinner Indian Style:
Vegetarian:
- Aloo Gobhi Masala - *Spicy Potato Cauliflower Curry – P80*
- Aloo Methi Masala - *Spicy Potato Fenugreek Curry– P81*
- Baingan Bhurta- *Eggplant Baba Ganoush – P85*
- Bhurma Karela – *Stuffed Bitter Gourd – P83*
- Khatta Meetha Kaddu – *Tangy Sweet Pumpkin – P94*
- Malai Kofta – *Vegetable Dumplings Curry – P96*
- Masala Bhindi - *Spicy Okra Curry – P99*
- Masala Choley – *Spicy Chick Pea Curry – P75*
- Masala Kaale Chaney - *Spicy Black Grams Curry – P77*
- Matar Paneer – *Peas Cottage Cheese Curry – P101*
- Mooli Baingan – *Radish Eggplant Curry – P103*
- Palak Paneer – *Spinach Cottage Cheese Curry – P105*
- Sarson Ka Saag – *Kale Spinach Collard Greens Curry – P109*

Non-Vegetarian:
- Keema Masala – *Spicy Mince Meat Curry – P152*
- Meat Kofta Curry – *Meat Ball Curry – P154*
- Murg Biryani – *Chicken Pilaf – P62*
- Murg Makhani– *Butter Chicken – P138*
- Nariyal Machchi– *Coconut Fish Curry – P145*
- Rogan Josh – *Lamb Curry – P156*
- Tandoori Murg – *Tandoori Chicken – P143*

Accompaniments:
- Aloo Raita– *Potato Yogurt Sauce – P58*
- Bhatura – *Deep Fried Puffed Bread – P168*
- Bhuna Papadam – *Roasted Lentil Cracker – P32*
- Boondi Raita – *Gram Flour Fried Puffs Yogurt Sauce– P58*
- Gajar Ki Kanji – *Carrot Beverage – P22*
- Ghiya Raita– *Bottle Gourd Yogurt Sauce– P58*
- Indian Naan – *Tandoori Flatbread– P175*
- Jal Zeera Pani – *Cumin Water– P20*
- Kheera Raita– *Cucumber Yogurt Sauce– P57*
- Mooli Lachcha – *Radish Relish – P30*
- Plain Kulcha – *Soft Roasted Flatbread– P178*
- Plain Parantha – *Plain Pan Fried Flatbread– P172*
- Podiney Ki Chutney – *Mint Chutney – P24*

Dinner Indian Style Contd.
Accompaniments:

- ➢ Podiney Ka Raita – *Mint Yogurt Sauce – P57*
- ➢ Pyaz Ka Lachcha – *Onion Relish – P31*
- ➢ Subzi Raita – *Vegetable Yogurt Sauce– P57*
- ➢ Tava Roti – *Griddle Roasted Wheat Flatbread – P166*
- ➢ Zafrani Chawal – *Savory Saffron Rice – P61*

Desserts Indian Style:
Vegetarian:

- Besan Burfi–*Gram Flour Fudge – P181*
- Chawal Kheer – *Rice Pudding – P186*
- Gajar Halwa – *Carrot Halwa - P184*
- Jalebi – *Indian Funnel Cake - P193*
- Nariyal Burfi – *Coconut Fudge – P182*
- Pista Kulfi – *Pistachio Ice Cream – P191*
- Rasgoola – *Sweet Cottage Cheese Dumplings – P188*

Index

Aam
   Mango, 15
Aam Ki Chutney
   Mango Chutney, 29
Aam Ki Kulfi
   Mango Kulfi, 192
Aam Ki Lassi
   Mango Smoothie, 15
Adrak
   Ginger, 11
Adrak-Hari Mirch
   Minced Ginger-Green Chili, 34
Ajwain
   Carom Seeds, 99
Al Dente
   Firmly Cooked, 49
Alfredo Florentine
   Spinach Pasta in White Sauce, 46
Aloo
   Potato, 34
Aloo Bonda
   Potato Dumplings, 125
Aloo Gobhi Masala
   Spicy Potato Cauliflower Curry, 80
Aloo Ka Bhurta
   Mashed Potatoes, 50
Aloo Khumbi Pulao
   Potato Mushroom Pilaf, 59
Aloo Matar Kulcha
   Potato Peas Soft Flatbread, 179
Aloo Methi Masala
   Spicy Potato Fenugreek Curry, 81
Aloo Pakora
   Potato Fritter, 116
Aloo Parantha
   Potato Stuffed Flatbread, 170
Aloo Raita
   Potato Yogurt Sauce, 58
Aloo Tikki
   Potato Cutlet, 113

Aloo Tikki Sandwich
   Potato Cutlet Sandwich, 42
Amchoor
   Mango Powder, 11
Anannāsa
   Pineapple, 197
Ararot
   Arrowroot Powder, 113
Arhar Dal
   Yellow Split Arhar Lentils, 66
Badam
   Almonds, 62
Badi Ilaichi
   Black Cardamom, 11
Baingan
   Eggplant, 39
Baingan Bhurta
   Eggplant Baba Ganoush, 85
Baingan Cutlet
   Eggplant Cutlet, 39
Baingan Lasagna
   Eggplant Lasagna, 48
Baingan Pakora
   Eggplant Fritter, 116
Baingan Palak Pizza
   Eggplant Spinach Pizza, 44
Baingan Parmesan
   Eggplant Parmesan, 87
Baingan Sandwich
   Eggplant Sandwich, 39
Baked Namak Paare
   Baked Savory Squares, 132
Banana Pistachio Bread, *195*
Bandgobhi
   Cabbage, 124
Bandgobhi Bonda
   Cabbage Dumplings, 124
Basmati Chawal
   Basmati Rice, 51

Besan
  Gram Flour, 91
Besan Burfi
  Gram Flour Fudge, 181
Besan Laddoo
  Gram Flour Sweet Balls, 181
Besan Pakori
  Gram Flour Dumplings, 108
Bhatura
  Fried Puffed Bread, 168
Bhindi
  Okra, 99
Bhuna Papadam
  Roasted Lentil Cracker, 32
Bhuna Zeera
  Roasted Cumin, 11, 14
Bhuni Machchi
  Grilled Fish, 148
Bhurma Baingan
  Stuffed Baby Eggplant, 89
Bhurma Bhatura
  Stuffed Puffed Bread, 169
Bhurma Karela
  Stuffed Bitter Gourd, 83
Boondi Raita
  Gram Flour Puffs Yogurt Sauce, 58
Chaunk/Baghar/Tadka
  Tempering, 67
Chawal Kheer
  Rice Pudding, 186
Chinese Okra
  Silk Squash, 98
Chini
  Sugar, 15
Chocolate Granola Squares, *198*
Chota Akhrot
  Pecans, 195
Choti Ilaichi
  Green Cardamom, 11
Cornish Pasty
  Meat Pie, 161

Dahi
  Yogurt, 15
Dahi Saunth Pakori
  Yogurt Tamarind Dumplings, 52
Dahi Vada
  Yogurt Lentil Doughnuts, 55
Dal
  Lentil, 66
Dal Palak
  Lentil Spinach Soup, 69
Dal Tadka
  Tempered Lentil Soup, 67
Dalchini
  Cinnamon, 11
Dalia
  Cream of Wheat, 123
Dhaniya
  Coriander, 11
Dosa
  Lentil Crepes, 66
'Dum'
  Cooked Over Low Heat, 62
ENO
  Fruit Salt, 119
Fruit Cookies, *197*
Gajar
  Carrot, 22
Gajar Halwa
  Carrot Pudding, 184
Gajar Kheer
  Carrot Milk Pudding, 185
Gajar Ki Kanji
  Carrot Beverage, 22
Garam Masala
  Mixed Spice, 13
Ghiya Raita
  Bottle Gourd Yogurt Sauce, 58
Gobhi
  Cauliflower, 37
Gobhi Makai Soup
  Cauliflower Corn Soup, 37

Gobhi Parantha
    Cauliflower Stuffed Flatbread, 172
Grilled Hash Sandwich, *137*
Gur
    Jaggery, 11
Haldi
    Turmeric, 11
Hara Pyaz
    Scallion, 42
Hari Mirch
    Green Chili, 11
Heeing
    Asafoetida, 11
How to Make Paneer
    How to Make Cottage Cheese, 111
Idli
    Steamed Lentil Rice Cake, 66
Imli
    Tamarind, 27
Imli Ki Chutney or Saunth
    Tamarind Chutney, 27
Imli Paste
    Tamarind Paste, 27
Indian Masale
    Indian Spices, 11
Indian Naan
    Tandoori Flatbread, 175
Jaiphal
    Nutmeg, 11
Jaitoon Ka Tel
    Olive Oil, 26
Jal Zeera Pani
    Cumin Water, 20
Jalebi
    Indian Funnel Cake, 193
Javitri
    Mace, 11
Jhaag
    Foam/White Substance , 72
'Josh'
    Intense Heat, 156

Kaale Chaney
    Black/Bengal Grams, 77
Kaddu
    Pumpkin, 94
Kadhi Pakori
    Gram Flour Dumplings Curry, 91
Kadi Patta
    Curry Leaf, 11
Kaju
    Cashews, 62
Kala Namak, pink in color
    Black Rock Salt, 20
Kali Gajar
    Black/Purple Carrot, 22
Kali Mirch
    Ground Black Pepper, 48
Khameer
    Active Dry Yeast, 175
Karela
    Bitter Gourd, 83
Karela Bhujia
    Bitter Gourd Curry, 84
Keema
    Mince Meat, 152
Keema Kulcha
    Keema Masala Soft Flatbread, 179
Keema Masala
    Spicy Minced Meat Curry, 152
Keema Parantha
    Keema Stuffed Flatbread, 173
Keema Samosa
    Keema Masala Stuffed Pastry, 130
Khatta Meetha Kaddu
    Tangy Sweet Pumpkin, 94
Kheera Raita
    Cucumber Yogurt Sauce, 57
Khichadi
    Lentil Rice Polenta, 64
Khoya
    Thickened Milk, 185
Khumbi Lobhiya Soup
    Mushroom Black-Eyed Pea Soup, 35

Kishmish
  Raisin, 195
Kurkuree Hari Phali
  Crispy Green Beans, 117
Lal Mirch
  Red Chili Powder, 24
Lal Mooli
  Red Radish, 30
Laung
  Clove, 11
Lehsun
  Garlic, 34
Lobhiya
  Black-Eyed Pea, 35
Machchi
  Fish, 145
Machchi Taco
  Fish Taco, 149
Makai
  Fresh Corn Kernels, 34
Makkhan
  Butter, 46
Makhane Ki Kheer
  Foxnut Pudding, 187
Malai Kofta
  Vegetable Dumplings Curry, 96
Masala Bhindi
  Spicy Okra Curry, 99
Masala Choley/Punjabi Choley
  Spicy Chick Pea Curry, 75
Masala Kaale Chaney
  Spicy Black Grams Curry, 77
Masoor Sabut
  Brown Whole Masoor Lentils, 66
Masoor Dhuli
  Red Split Masoor Lentils, 66
Matar
  Green Peas, 101
Matar Paneer
  Peas Cottage Cheese Curry, 101
Matthi
  Pastry Crisps, 130
Meat Kofta
  Meat Balls, 155

Meat Kofta Curry
  Meat Balls Curry, 154
Meetha Dalia
  Sweet Cream of Wheat, 123
Methi Parantha
  Fenugreek Stuffed Flatbread, 172
Methi Beej
  Fenugreek Seeds, 11
Methi/ Kasoori Methi
  Dry Fenugreek Leaves, 81
Mooli Aloo Hash
  Radish Potato Hash, 104
Mooli Baingan
  Radish Eggplant Curry, 103
Mooli Bhujia
  Radish Greens Curry, 104
Mooli Lachcha
  Radish Relish, 30
Mooli Parantha
  Radish Stuffed Flatbread, 173
Moong Chilka
  Green Split Moong Lentils, 66
Moong Dal Pakori
  Moong Lentil Dumplings, 51
Murg
  Chicken, 62
Murg Biryani
  Chicken Pilaf, 62
Murg Makhani
  Butter Chicken, 138
Murg Pie
  Chicken Pie, 159
Murg Tikka Masala
  Spicy Chicken Tikka, 141
Namak
  Salt, 15
Nariyal
  Coconut, 182
Nariyal Burfi
  Coconut Fudge, 182
Nariyal Machchi
  Coconut Fish Curry, 145
Neembu
  Lime, Lemon, 17, 24

Neembu Cheeley
Lemon Crepes, 126
Neembu Pani
Fresh Lemonade, 17
Neembu Rus
Lime or Lemon Juice, 17
Pakori
Dumplings, 51
Palak
Spinach, 105
Palak Methi Kulcha
Spinach Fenugreek Soft Flatbread, 179
Palak Paneer
Spinach Cottage Cheese Curry, 105
Palak Parantha
Spinach Stuffed Flatbread, 173
Paneer
Cottage Cheese, 111
Paneer Ki Kheer
Cottage Cheese Pudding, 189
Paneer Ki Roti
Cottage Cheese Roasted Flatbread, 112
Paneer Kofta
Cheese Dumplings, 102
Paneer Kulcha
Cottage Cheese Soft Flatbread, 179
Papadam
Lentil Cracker, 32
Pista
Pistachio, 191
Pista Kulfi
Pistachio Ice Cream, 191
Plain Khoya Burfi
Plain Milk Fudge, 183
Plain Kulcha
Soft Roasted Flatbread, 178
Plain Parantha
Plain Pan Fried Flatbread, 172
Podina Raita
Mint Yogurt Sauce, 57
Podiney Ki Chutney
Mint Chutney, 24

Podiney Ki Lassi
Savory Mint Smoothie, 17
Pyaz
Onion, 24
Pyaz Ka Lachcha
Onion Relish, 31
Pyaz Kulcha
Onion Soft Flatbread, 179
Pyaz Pakora
Onion Fritter, 116
Rai
Mustard Seeds, 11
Rajbhog
Sweet Stuffed Rasgoola, 189
Rajma
Red Kidney Beans, 73
Rajma Curry
Red Kidney Beans Curry, 73
Ras Malai
Rasgoola in Sweet Milk Syrup, 189
Rasa Pakori
Lentil Dumplings Curry, 107
Rasgoola
Sugar Syrup Dumplings , 188
Rava
Roasted Semolina, 121
'Rogan'
Oil, 156
Rogan Josh
Lamb Curry, 156
Roux
Mixture of Flour and Fat, 47
Sabut Gol Lal Mirch
Red Whole Round Chili, 13
Sabut Kali Mirch
Whole Peppercorn, 11
Subzi Pakora
Vegetable Fritter, 115
Subzi Raita
Vegetable Yogurt Sauce, 57
Subzi Roll
Vegetable Roll, 134

Subzi Rus
  Vegetable Juice, 35
Sabut Urad Dal
  Black Whole Urad Lentil, 66
Sada Chaunk
  Plain Tempering, 68
Sarson Ka Saag
  Kale Spinach Collard Greens Curry, 109
Saunf
  Fennel Seeds, 11
Sausage Roll
  Meat Roll, 163
Seared Machchi
  Pan Seared Fish, 150
Sevian Kheer
  Indian Vermicelli Pudding, 187
Shakarkandi
  Sweet Potato, 136
Shakarkandi Makai Hash
  Sweet Potato Corn Hash, 136
Shehad
  Honey, 17
Shimla Mirch
  Bell Pepper, 34
Shimla Mirch Makai Soup
  Bell Pepper Corn Soup, 34
Sirka
  Vinegar, 26
Sooji
  Semolina, 119
Sooji Dhokla
  Savory Semolina Cake, 119
Sooji Upma
  Semolina Polenta, 121
Sukhi Urad
  Tempered Dry Urad Lentils, 71
Tandoori Machchi
  Broiled Fish, 147

Tandoori Murg
  Tandoori Chicken, 143
Tandoori Roti
  Tandoor Baked Flatbread, 167
Tava
  Cast Iron Griddle, 166
Tava Roti
  Griddle Roasted Wheat Flatbread, 166
Tej Patta
  Bay Leaf, 11
Timatar
  Tomato, 26
Timatar Ki Chutney
  Tomato Chutney, 26
Timatar Rus
  Tomato Juice, 34
Tortilla Samosa
  Vegetable Stuffed Tortilla, 130
Urad Dal Vada
  Urad Lentil Doughnut, 51
Urad Dhuli
  White Split Urad Lentil, 66
Vegetable Samosa
  Vegetable Stuffed Pastry, 128
'Whey'
  Water from Cottage Cheese, 111
White Choley
  Chick Peas, 75
White Sauce
  Bechamel Sauce, 47
Zafran
  Saffron, 61
Zafrani Chawal
  Savory Saffron Rice, 61
Zeera
  Cumin Seeds, 14

Thank You

Made in the USA
Middletown, DE
02 September 2024